# Leopard Geckos

Gerold Merker and Cindy Merker
with Julie Bergman and Tom Mazorlig

# Leopard Geckos

Project Team
Editor: Thomas Mazorlig
Copy Editor: Mary Grangeia
Cover Design: Cándida Moreira Tómassini, Mary Ann Kahn
Design: Patti Escabi

T.F.H. Publications
President/CEO: Glen S. Axelrod
Executive Vice President: Mark E. Johnson
Publisher: Christopher T. Reggio
Production Manager: Kathy Bontz

T.F.H. Publications, Inc.
One TFH Plaza
Third and Union Avenues
Neptune City, NJ 07753

Printed and bound in China,

10 11 12 13 14     7 9 11 13 12 10 8

**Library of Congress Cataloging-in-Publication Data**
Leopard geckos : a complete guide to eublepharine geckos / Gerold Merker ... [et al.].
p. cm.
Includes bibliographical references and index.
ISBN 0-7938-2883-X (alk. paper)
1. Leopard geckos as pets. I. Merker, Gerold.
SF459.G35L46 2006
639.3'952--dc22
2005035329

*The Leader In Responsible Animal Care For Over 50 Years!®*
www.tfh.com

# Table of Contents

**G**eckos, especially terrestrial species, have fascinated me since my youth. However, at that time, there was no way of knowing that geckos would remain a part of my life and become a career. My experience and resultant fascination with geckos was based on an early encounter with a handful of individuals of a single species—the western banded gecko, *Coleonyx variegatus*. Restriction to a single species was not a desire, but a reality. Geckos could only be had by capturing them yourself, and the only one within my reach was of the local variety. Despite my youthful naiveté, I succeeded in not only maintaining this species, but also breeding it. My interest in expanding hands-on knowledge to a greater variety of terrestrial geckos was great, but the means were inadequate. Exposure to other species would have to be limited to oohing and ahhing at pictures, and hoping that the future would lead to growing opportunities to work with them.

I wish all my hopes and dreams in life came to fruition like those about these geckos. Over the past few decades, I have gone from defending my animals from feeder-lizard hungry snake keepers to sharing my interests with an enormous number of fellow enthusiasts. I have been able to maintain a large variety of geckos that even my greatest hopes during youth did not include. I have admired these captivating animals in their natural environments on four continents and contributed to the scientific literature pertaining to this group of animals. While my fascination for these animals has not changed, my experiences surely have.

# Foreword

It is with this background that I welcome and truly admire the contributions that Gerold and Cindy Merker make to the herpetological literature. As with their previous works, Gerold and Cindy reflect years of experience that will be of great benefit to the ever-growing population of gecko enthusiasts. They have put together an easy to read text that provides highly relevant and useful information that will maximize the reader's potential as a hobbyist. With the help of this valuable resource, successfully maintaining terrestrial geckos can be a reality for almost anyone. Throughout the book, the authors provide the necessary details on care and emphasize the commitments that must be adhered to in order to achieve the desired outcome. Their years of personal experience provide a strong foundation for their writing, and they openly seek assistance from others to strengthen the quality of their work. In this book, Gerold and Cindy include valuable contributions from Julie Bergman and Tom Mazorlig to effectively cover a broad range of commonly kept terrestrial geckos. While factual treasures always reside in the text, everyone knows that a book on reptile herpetoculture without photographs is a book that will go mostly unread. Photo enthusiasts will not be disheartened by this effort. Gerold's photography skills are well demonstrated in this book, providing a great representation of the exceptional diversity of leopard geckos and similar species that exist.

While there is nothing like seeing these exciting creatures in their native habitats, this book offers the next best thing – beautiful images that allow even the novice to enjoy these animals close up for years.

Dale DeNardo

*Assistant Professor and University Veterinarian, Arizona State University in Tempe*

O ver the past three decades, there has been a dramatic rise in the popularity of eublepharine geckos in general and the leopard gecko specifically. There are many reasons these geckos became popular, including their appealing appearance, the ease of maintaining these animals in captivity, and the wide variety of species and color morphs available.

There is some argument as to the classification of eublepharine geckos. The most widely accepted phylogenetic relationship describes the Eublepharinae as a subfamily of the Gekkonidae (Bartlett, 1997). However, the taxonomy of eublepharine geckos depends upon the source describing them. They have also been classified as a subfamily (Eublepharinae) within their own superfamily (Eublepharoidea) according to Kluge (1987).

The hallmark of this group of geckos is their lidded eyes. All species of eublepharine gecko lack toe pads on their feet. Many species within the Gekkonidae have clear spectacles over the eye, whereas eublepharine geckos have true eyelids. They are nocturnal and, for the most part, inhabit arid and sub-humid environments. However, as with any rule, there are some exceptions to this. The Central American banded gecko, *Coleonyx mitratus*, and the elegant gecko, *Coleonyx elegans*, are found in tropical environments. An even more interesting microhabitat is where the Japanese leopard gecko, *Goniurosaurus kuroiwae*, is found. These medium-sized geckos live in moist environments, particularly caves in the Ryukyu Archipelago of Asia (Frantz, 1992). With the exception of one arboreal species from Southeast Asia, *Aeluroscalabotes felinus*, all species of eublepharine gecko are terrestrial (Pough

# Introduction

et al., 2004). As a group, these geckos have a disjunctive distribution, with species occurring in parts of both the Old World and the New World. Their range includes Japan, North America, Central America, Africa, and Southeast Asia, including Afghanistan, Pakistan, and India.

There are six recognized genera and approximately 20 species within the subfamily Eublepaharinae (Pough et al., 2004). Some species, such as the leopard gecko, *Eublepharis macularius*, mature quickly, reaching adult size in less than a year. Most species are sexually dimorphic and the gender is easily discerned in adults, as males possess a distinct row of femoral pores above the vent. In some, like the banded geckos, *Coleonyx*, males have easily discernible spurs on either side of their vents.

This book outlines proven strategies to successfully maintain some of the more popular species of eublepharine gecko, including leopard geckos, *Eublepharis macularius*, banded geckos, *Coleonyx* sp., and African fat-tailed geckos, *Hemitheconyx caudicinctus*. Included are tips for proper caging, feeding, and breeding of these species. Important information about successful feeding strategies and hiding areas are highlighted using sidebars. Also included in this book is information on some of the popular pattern and color morphs exhibited by eublepharine geckos, particularly those found in leopard geckos. Proven strategies to diagnose and treat many diseases commonly found in these lizards are also provided. The authors have extensive experience with many of the species and will provide many personal accounts of what has been successful for them, as well as providing information on the strategies employed by other gecko enthusiasts.

# Chapter 1

# Leopard Geckos as Pets

eopard geckos make very interesting subjects for both professional herpetologists and amateur keepers. They are usually friendly, highly adaptable to captivity, and can possess a beautiful pattern. Leopard geckos do not become very large and thus do not require a large cage for their maintenance. This is a useful characteristic for people with limited living space. They will thrive for years on food sources that are readily obtainable, including crickets or mealworms. Because they are a temperate species, they acclimate very easily. Also, they do not have an ultraviolet light requirement. Taking into account all these characteristics, care of leopard geckos is much less demanding, so they make better candidates for captivity than some of the other exotic lizard species like chameleons, iguanas, or monitors.

Leopard geckos are popular with hobbyists because they are beautiful, docile, and easy to care for.

If you desire an animal that will respond like a cat or a dog, then the leopard gecko may not be for you. They will, however, respond in a manner indicating that they recognize you. If you open the cage, many leopard geckos will immediately wander over to inspect what you are doing and may actually climb up on your hand. They are probably hoping for some food! There is also a wide variation in personality. Some of our leopard geckos squeal with discontent every time you look at them or attempt to work in their enclosure. Fortunately, this behavior is uncommon. They are usually very friendly and do accommodate interaction with their human keepers. Most leopard geckos are reluctant to bite and will usually only do so with extreme provocation, such as being restrained for medical treatment, etc.

## Natural History of Leopard Geckos

The genus name of the leopard gecko, *Eublepharis*, is derived from Greek and indicates a well-made or typical eyelid (Balsai, 1993; de Vosjoli et al., 2004). The Latin species name *macularius* refers to the spots typical of this gecko (Balsai, 1993).

Leopard geckos range in the wild from northern India, Pakistan, and possibly Afghanistan (Balsai, 1993). There are about four or five species in the genus *Eublepharis* (Balsai, 1993). Leopard geckos are terrestrial and spend most daylight hours in the comfort of their underground homes. They live in arid regions, including grasslands, with substantial cover (Hiduke and Bryant, 2003). According to de Vosjoli et al. (2004), the earlier stock of leopard geckos was imported from Pakistan, and later on from Afghanistan. The first animals imported commanded high prices.

## Description

Leopard geckos are medium-sized geckos ranging up to 8 inches (20.4 cm) in total length. As babies, they are approximately 3.5 inches (8 cm) in length. In general, they reach adult size fairly swiftly, often in less than a year. The head is similar to that of most geckos; that is, they have a triangular head with a distinct neck. As with all eublepharine lizards, they have a well-developed eyelid.

The skin of a leopard gecko has a "bumpy" appearance due to small tubercles on the surface of the skin. Their common name is derived from the spotted pattern that adults have. The background color can range from a muddy gray to a bright yellow to a brilliant yellow, depending on the color morph. The spots are usually a darker brown; they also afford the gecko some concealment from predators.

## Taxonomy of Leopard Geckos

**Kingdom: Animalia**
**Phylum: Chordata**
**Subphylum: Vertebrata**
**Class: Reptilia**
**Order: Squamata**
**Suborder: Sauria**
**Infraorder: Gekkota**
**Family: Gekkonidae**
**Subfamily: Eublepharinae**
**Genus: *Eublepharis***
**Species: *macularius***

The bumps in the skin of leopard geckos are called tubercles.

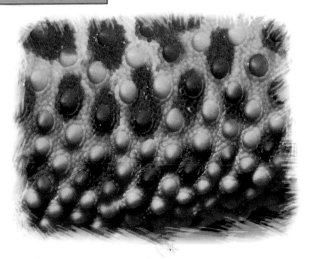

## Purchasing a Leopard Gecko

Leopard geckos, although not as expensive to keep in the long term as a cat or dog, do require some cost for their care. The initial outlay of money for the cage, cage heater, substrate, and hiding area is something to take into consideration when purchasing a leopard gecko. That cost may run into the hundreds of dollars depending upon how elaborate the owner wants to get. A cage setup can be done cheaply if the appearance of the enclosure is not too important or if you are able to acquire caging second hand. Also, if veterinarian assistance is required, that could become very expensive. As with any pet, the cost of food is always part of the equation. Heating costs also need to be considered, although a leopard gecko's heating requirements are modest. To properly keep your new acquisition at appropriate temperatures, you will have to spend some money on power. Like a dog or cat, a leopard gecko may live well into its teens or even early 20's.

## Leopard Gecko Sources

There are several sources to consider when purchasing a leopard gecko. The local pet store is a great place to purchase one, if the personnel in the store understand the captive maintenance of these animals and are well versed in their nutritional and habitat requirements. Also, if there is a problem with your gecko later on, you should be able to bring him back to your local pet store for assistance if the staff is properly educated. If they do not appear knowledgeable or the store appears sub-par—dirty cages, poor lighting, smells bad, unhealthy animals—this may not be the place to purchase your pet.

When purchasing your pet from a breeder on the Internet, inquiry may not be a possibility. However, by buying your gecko online, you may be getting the animal from the same source as your local pet store. That translates to acquiring your new pet at a reduced cost if shipping fees are not too steep. You may want to explore the reputation of the breeder before purchasing a leopard gecko from them. This can be accomplished by asking other hobbyists about their experiences buying from breeders online or by locating

# Autotomy

A healthy leopard gecko has a fat tail that will break off if the lizard is mishandled. Called autotomy, this is an adaptation to ensure escape from predation. When the tail falls off, it wriggles for some time attracting the attention of the predator, which allows time for the gecko to escape. Eventually, the tail will grow back. However, the regenerated tail is never as beautiful as the original. The tail also acts as an energy storage organ.

Like many other lizards, leopard geckos can lose their tails as a defensive mechanism.

one of the many online forums that discuss these types of issues.

A reptile show (also called a herp expo) is another place to consider purchasing a leopard gecko. At most of the shows currently taking place, there is a wide array of animals from which to choose, and many different pattern and color morphs can be seen. A lot of reptile shows also exhibit the "price war" phenomenon, which may ensure fairly reasonable costs. However, you often get what you pay for. If you come across a beautiful leopard gecko at a ridiculously low price, there may be a reason for it. These reasons can include the seller wanting to dispose of an old breeder, or worse, a very sick animal.

## Selecting a Healthy Pet

Examine the health of the gecko before purchasing the animal. Saving a few dollars during the initial purchase may not offset the money spent

Breeders produce many interesting and beautiful leopard geckos (such as this tangerine) for the pet trade.

at the veterinary clinic trying to heal a sick animal. Keep in mind that if problems arise later with your new lizard, it may be difficult to seek monetary restitution if the person from whom you purchased the animal is across the country or in a different country altogether.

There are many important factors to take into account before you purchase your pet. Here's a detailed list of what to look for:

• **Check out the facility (private breeder or store) selling the leopard gecko.**

Is the establishment clean? Does the store seem to be staffed with knowledgeable people? Are the cages of an appropriate size, with only one or a few animals per cage? Are the geckos guaranteed for a small period of time so that you may ascertain their health?

• **See if the animals that you are interested in purchasing are receiving proper care.**

Have the lizards been placed in a safe cage that sets up a healthy situation for them? Is the cage, for instance, clean of feces? Are there regurgitations from improperly sized food items? Are there hide boxes? Obviously, the staff selling the leopard gecko may know little about the natural history of these animals if they have them set up in a "shore-line" habitat.

• **Examine the gecko in the cage and be sure that it looks healthy.**

A leopard gecko that has received improper care is easily discerned. A healthy gecko should have lustrous skin. If it has trouble shedding, old pieces of skin may be attached to the animal. Again, this implies improper care, or it also may indicate the animal is unhealthy. A skinny tail indicates disease or lack of food. If the tail is skinny and the gecko has protruding hipbones, do not purchase the animal as this also suggests that it is not feeding well on its own or that the store is not feeding it enough. Look at the eyes: are they clear, open, and healthy-looking? Does the animal have a rubbed rostral (nose) scale? All these factors point to an unhealthy animal that should be avoided at all costs. A healthy gecko should be alert and have an eager appetite. His tail and body should be full, although not necessarily fat. The limbs and body should be strong, not limp or showing signs of breaks. Feces around the cloaca could indicate diarrhea, a possible sign of disease.

A leopard gecko may vary in price depending upon the animal's color and size. Also, where you purchase the gecko can influence the cost. Seemingly good deals can be seen on the Internet or at reptile shows. However, if you purchase from a breeder living a great distance

When a leopard gecko loses its tail, the regenerated one is often misshapen in some way.

from your home, shipping and boxing costs to get the animal safely to you will substantially escalate the total amount spent on the animal. Keep in mind, there are many different places from which to purchase a leopard gecko. Once you have determined the facility from which you want to make your purchase, go ahead and do so. Do not try to save an animal that is certain to die. The result is usually unhappiness for all parties concerned, except the unscrupulous vendor that received the money for his or her unhealthy animal.

**A Growing Health Issue** Very few leopard geckos are imported, which means that the ones that are currently available are captive bred. In most cases, captive-bred reptiles do not harbor the parasites that are frequently seen in wild-caught animals. In recent years, however, there has been a disconcerting trend of captive-bred leopard geckos hosting the protozoan *Cryptosporidium* (known as "crypto" to hobbyists). Lizards afflicted with this parasite often demonstrate a "wasting away" appearance. The prognosis is grim for these animals, even though there have been advancements made in the understanding and treatment of it (see diseases section).

If the store from which you are considering making your purchase has their leopard geckos grouped together, evaluate their condition carefully. If some look healthy and

If you purchase an animal that is unhealthy because you feel badly for it, you have only helped perpetuate a lack of care for these animals by breeders and sellers. The kind but difficult approach is to refuse to purchase an animal in poor condition in the hopes that, over time, overall circumstances will improve for future generations of captive animals. Make sure you politely tell the vendor that you are taking your business elsewhere because of the unhealthy animals offered for sale.

others appear emaciated, turn around and exit the store. Even though an animal looks healthy, it may still have *Cryptosporidium*. If you purchase an additional healthy animal in the future and place it in the terrarium with the first diseased gecko you purchased, the consequences will be dire.

There may be some breeders who, through carelessness or lack of ethics, sell animals infected with *Cryptosporidium*. The animals they sell then infect healthy animals with which they come into contact. The unsuspecting customer purchases an infected animal and cares for it properly, only to have it slowly deteriorate and eventually die. This may give the leopard gecko the undeserved reputation of being difficult to care for in captivity. In actuality, leopard geckos are one of the easiest reptiles to care for in captivity and the animal was likely doomed before its purchase.

## Bringing Your Leopard Gecko Home

### The Journey Home

You made your big purchase and now the animal is yours! The first concern is safely transporting your leopard gecko home. A very important item to ensure that the animal makes it home safely is an ice chest. If the weather is chilly, a chemical heat pack may be used in the ice chest to prevent the gecko from becoming too cold. During the heat of the summer, an ice pack can be used to maintain safe temperatures. Also, the dark in the ice chest will prevent the gecko from becoming stressed during his ride from the warm environs of the store to your home.

### Acclimatization

The first few days at your home are vitally important for the proper acclimatization of your new ward. A prudent idea is to have the cage you plan to keep your gecko in set up

Newly acquired leopard geckos should not be handled for the first few days, so that they can adjust to their new surroundings.

prior to his arrival. This means that any cage heater used should be adjusted properly so that the temperature in the cage allows him to thrive. He should be placed into the new cage with minimal disturbance. If the new gecko is like any other animal placed into a new environment, he will check out his new home. This means he will inspect different regions of the cage, which may involve some licking of the various new perch sites, water bowls, or hiding areas. This is not the time to constantly take your new ward out and hold him. You may want to offer some food items to him during the next day or so. If he eats one food item, try another. Do not feed your gecko too much at this time in order to prevent regurgitation, which will increase the stress the animal is experiencing.

## Quarantine

If you have other leopard geckos, you definitely will want to quarantine your new pet to prevent any diseases from being spread from your new gecko to the other geckos in your collection. Practice safe hygiene with all the animals by diligently washing your hands after holding them or cleaning fecal matter from the cage. This is an important practice in order to prevent diseases from spreading to your other reptiles or perhaps even to you. A period of 30 to 60 days works very well for quarantine. This may be the time to have a qualified veterinarian perform a fecal test on fresh excreta. If your new gecko is adjusting well to its captive conditions, it probably does not have anything that could harm your other reptile pets.

# Chapter 2

# Housing

A leopard gecko represents a long-term investment of both your time and money. These animals are very long-lived if they receive proper care. Remember, after the initial investment for the animal, there are also the cage, substrate, heater, and food and water dishes to consider. Furthermore, feeding your pet can represent a substantial amount of money over the course of the life of the gecko.

## Separate the Boys

As long as you have enough space in the enclosure, you should have no problem housing a small group of leopard geckos together. However, if more than one of those geckos is a male, there will be problems. When the males become mature, they will start fighting. You may not see them skirmish, but you will see the bite wounds and missing tails. To avoid this, house only one male per enclosure.

The beauty of keeping leopard geckos in captivity is that they do so well in almost any cage setup imaginable. As long as their basic needs are met, they will survive in the simplest of caging systems. A naturalistic setup also works for the more discriminating keeper of these desert jewels. Building the perfect habitat for your lizard can take on the range of these extremes. Various types of habitat are available for leopard geckos.

## Types of Habitat

### Simple Enclosures

Our leopard geckos are kept under very simple conditions. We keep our animals in small Freedom Breeder reptile enclosures. This form of caging works very well because it is well ventilated. The cage heater is placed toward the back, which sets up an excellent temperature gradient. The lizards can choose to be at approximately 86°F (30°C) on the warm end to approximately 70°F (21°C) on the cool end. This thermal gradient sets up conditions that allow the animal to choose his own temperature. More often than not, the animals will be found toward the cooler end of the cage.

For substrate, we use one of the calcium/sand products available in pet stores. As with Tremper (2000), we do not recommend the use of sand with younger animals to avoid impaction.

Cage furniture is very simple, as well, consisting of a shallow water dish and a paper towel tube for a hiding area. Under these conditions, we have kept one animal for over six years with no problems.

### Mid-Level Enclosures

For most leopard gecko keepers, a cage based upon a 10-gallon (38 l) aquarium will work very well. This size enclosure will provide your pet with ample room to move about and can be designed to look very attractive to both the animal inside the cage and the humans on the outside. It will also provide enough room to house a pair of leopard geckos. Make sure that you never keep two males in the same enclosure because both will engage in fighting. We have seen the results of such altercations, the worst of which will certainly result in amputation of damaged limbs. Furthermore, it is wise to provide ample hiding areas so that the animals can feel comfortable in the enclosure.

A substrate of sand works very well with adult leopard geckos, but again, should be avoided for young animals for fear that they may ingest it accidentally and become impacted with sand. Sand is a great substrate because it allows gradual temperature increases and decreases.

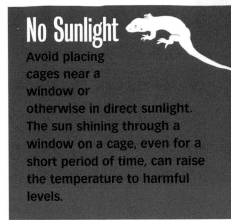

## No Sunlight

Avoid placing cages near a window or otherwise in direct sunlight. The sun shining through a window on a cage, even for a short period of time, can raise the temperature to harmful levels.

As in small enclosures, some form of heater must be incorporated to allow for temperature gradients to be set up in the cage. Many different types of heating systems can be used. A heater (heat tape, a light, or an undertank heating pad) with some form of controller to prevent overheating is essential. The controller can be either a thermostat, which is best, or a tabletop dimmer. Frequent checking with a thermometer ensures that the cage, hence the animal, does not become overheated. As with the simple enclosure, you want to set up a temperature range of about 86°F (30°C) to approximately 70°F (21°C).

A screened top works well for keeping the geckos in and keeping the other house pets, like cats, out. Because geckos have nocturnal

As long as their needs are met, leopard geckos will thrive in very simple enclosures.

Here is a simple but complete setup for a leopard gecko. It contains food and water bowls, hiding places, heat, substrate, and a secure cage top.

behaviors, a light on top of the cage is purely cosmetic and is not necessary; however, it does increase the keeper's enjoyment of observing the lizard.

## The Naturalistic Setup

For some keepers of leopard geckos, there is an intense desire to fabricate the ultimate enclosure that will be enjoyed by both the keeper and the gecko. Leopard geckos are excellent candidates for a naturalistic environment because of their size. They are not so large that they would cause harmful rearrangement to the contents of the terrarium. Furthermore, their feces are easily removed from the enclosure due to their dry nature.

**The Enclosure** We have visited many people who have wonderful setups for their geckos. Most of these cages are composed of a large 30- to 40-gallon (113.6 to 151.4 l) glass aquarium. However, there are many other options for the base cage as is evident at every reptile show across the nation. As part of their caging line, many manufacturers of reptile enclosures have some form of display cage. They all work remarkably well.

The glass aquarium is a good choice because it is readily available and cost savings are usually substantial. We have been at numerous shows marveling at the many enclosures specifically designed for reptiles. Usually, at that same show we see very nice large glass aquariums offered at a fraction of the cost of a similarly sized enclosure that is specifically manufactured for reptiles. These aquariums work as well as the other enclosures, and they offer several advantages. One is the fact that they are waterproof. The others may claim that they are waterproof, but in our experience they will leak over time. A waterproof enclosure is necessary if you are planning to keep plants in the cage. Unfortunately, the glass enclosure has a disadvantage, which is its fragile nature. Glass aquariums are broken easily during cleaning, or if rocks are carelessly moved about during construction of a natural environment.

**Substrate and Rocks** In designing your naturalistic enclosure, installing the undertank heater is the first step. After that, place the drainage layer on the bottom of the cage. It is best to use an inch or two of porous rock for this bottom layer (de Vosjoli, 1996). Next come the larger rocks, which are placed on top of the porous layer. This is essential. You do not want to place the rocks on the top layer, which is sand. Even a small animal like a leopard gecko can dig under the rock. If there is sand under the rock, the leopard gecko may dig enough out to get crushed under the weight of it. Also, you may want to add some wood branches to the enclosures. Although they do not climb often, leopard geckos occasionally use them in their enclosures. Avoid the artificial branches. These are often hollow, with access holes at the bottom. It would not be unrealistic to find that a gecko could get into the branch by way of this hole, and extracting the animal could be a problem.

After you have the rocks and branches where you want them, place a layer of sand several inches in depth around the rocks and branches. The sand has several important

Rocks can be used to make the enclosure appear more natural and give the gecko (a patternless individual is shown) climbing and hiding areas.

functions. First, it will collect the fecal matter. Second, sand distributes the heat in the enclosure. It acts as a heat sink so that when the lights turn off, it will remain warm for several hours after "sunset."

**Plants** If you want to use plants in the enclosure, place them around the cage in small pots, which will hold moisture so that the keeper will not have to water the entire enclosure. The best plants to use in a desert cage include various species of snake plants (*Sansevieria*), caudiciforms, ponytail palms, caudxed figs, bromeliads (our favorite), and euphoribias (de Vosjoli, 1996). One does not want to overdo the plants, in part, for ease of cleaning the enclosure. Even though leopard geckos do not need UV light, the plants will. A full spectrum fluorescent light works well to provide them with the UV radiation they need to grow and flourish, and it will not harm the animals.

**Feeding Stations** Placement of feeding stations is also important in the design of the naturalistic cage. A typical feeding station consists of a very shallow dish. The advantage of using such a station is that it prevents live food from escaping and causing problems for a sleeping gecko. In the past, we have had the problem of some of our lizards being fed upon by mealworms that have escaped being eaten by the lizard. This is especially true of the "super" mealworms, *Zoophobas morio*. The keeper of the leopard gecko can help to ameliorate this difficulty by only offering enough food for the lizards to feed upon at one time.

The feeding station also allows the keeper to easily supplement the food items with a mineral/vitamin/calcium supplement. Simply place the supplement in the container and then place the crickets or mealworms inside of it. As they move around in the container, the food items will have some of the supplement adhere to their exoskeleton. Having a feeding station that fits in with the naturalistic cage and is easily accessible to the keeper are things that need to be considered when building the enclosure.

Crickets usually escape feeding stations easily. It is best to feed crickets and similar feeders in small numbers that your geckos will consume in a few minutes. Remove any uneaten insects daily.

Calcium-based sand is one of several safe and effective substrate choices.

**Cleaning** An important consideration when designing a naturalistic enclosure is ease of cleaning. Removing leopard gecko scats is accomplished easily in a basic type of enclosure. However, the naturalistic setup adds a new dimension to cage cleaning because the fastidiousness of

## Authors' Preference

We use red sand from Utah. It looks beautiful and does not seem to stick to the animal even when wet. This is available in pet stores that specialize in herps, through online retailers, and at herp shows.

these animals will help facilitate this process. A healthy leopard gecko has very dry feces. This, coupled with the animal's habit of using the same region of the cage for depositing feces, will allow the keeper to easily clean up after his or her ward. You can use the same substrate for months. All you have to do is use a spoon to scoop up droppings and occasionally replace the substrate that has been removed during cleanup. Depending on the number of geckos you keep, substrate should be entirely replaced every few months, however.

## Substrate

Choosing the correct substrate to use on the bottom of the cage is a critical step for ensuring the long-term survival of your leopard gecko. There are many substrates from which to choose, including sand that is safe for reptiles, newspaper, paper toweling, Astroturf, and mulch.

Substrates such as pine shavings and especially cedar shavings should be avoided. They may become lodged in the mouths of geckos after catching a food item and later lead to problems. Furthermore, cedar shavings are known to cause toxic reactions in reptiles.

Sand is an excellent substrate. The advantage of using it is that it acts as a superior heat distributor. Also, it is easy to clean using one of the devices utilized for sifting sand available at many pet stores. Sand is also pleasing to the viewer's eye. The type utilized needs to have grains that are not too sharp (like the type used for sand blasting). This is to prevent problems when the lizard accidentally ingests some of the substrate during feeding. The disadvantage of sand is that younger geckos could ingest too much of it with food items and develop intestinal impactions (Tremper, 2000). Playground sand and sands that are manufactured for use in reptile enclosures should be safe for your gecko. Misting the sand will also prevent ingestion because it will form a hardened layer when it dries.

Newspaper is inexpensive, easily replaced, and safe, but it is unattractive. Furthermore, it should be replaced frequently to prevent a buildup of feces. Paper towels work well with young leopard geckos. They also are easily replaced when soiled, readily available, and will not cause the intestinal impaction problems mentioned with sand. Astroturf also has advantages, but most keepers will find that it is not esthetically pleasing. Also, mulch is very absorbent, and it looks attractive; however, mulch is not cleaned as easily as sand. Whatever substrate is used, it is vital to keep the material as clean as possible, whether that means replacing it altogether or removing the feces on a regular basis. It should be pointed out that some breeders recommend no substrate be utilized in the cage design. This is to prevent bacteria from building up in the enclosure and also to prevent impeding the gecko from getting vitamin and mineral supplements. In this system, to clean the cage, remove the leopard geckos and place them in a plastic container with small air holes. Then remove all the cage furniture and simply vacuum out the feces and excreta. Use a dampened paper towel to wipe out the cage and then replace the lizards.

## Shavings Are Bad Substrate

**Do not use wood shavings as the substrate in your gecko enclosure. They are easily ingested with food items and can cause problems with your pet's gastrointestinal tract. Cedar shavings should be avoided due to their toxic nature. They have been demonstrated to release toxic fumes leading to, among other things, neurological damage to reptiles.**

## Cage Furniture

Hiding places are critical for the well-being of your gecko.

With many species of lizard, the items (or lack of items) placed in the cage are important to the survival of that lizard under captive conditions. In reality, leopard geckos have very simple requirements for living in captivity. An important factor to their well-being is a hiding area. Leopard geckos definitely appreciate a darkened retreat in their enclosures. The hide box can be as simple as cardboard tubing from a paper towel roll. A plastic container with a hole on the side or the top of it also works well. A lot of manufacturers of reptile products have special hide boxes for lizards in their product lines. These also work well. Some have an elaborate design that, when placed next to the glass side of the enclosure, allows the keeper to view the leopard gecko inside the hide area.

As simple as it sounds, the implementation of a hiding area in your leopard gecko enclosure can add years to the

## Paper and Sand

Purchased in bulk, sand is a good substrate choice in many ways, especially for larger leopard geckos. There is always a concern that some sand will be ingested when the gecko feeds, but if it is not sharp, this is usually not a problem. For younger specimens, white paper toweling is an excellent choice. Both sand and paper towels are easily cleaned and are usually less problematic than other substrates.

life of your pet. Security is central to its long-term health. Allowing the lizard a retreat that is moist and dark will increase its feelings of safety. One of the most important benefits of an increased feeling of security will be the likelihood of a strong feeding response. Also, a retreat with increased humidity will ensure that your leopard gecko will shed its skin properly.

A plastic container with a circular opening twice the diameter of the lizard's body cut into its side will suffice as a hiding area. The entrance should be about 2 inches (5 cm) from the bottom of the container. This will keep most of the substrate from falling out of it. Inside the container, place some damp vermiculite or sand at a depth of almost 2 inches (5cm). Even paper towels will work, but they will need more frequent replacement. A long, thin hiding area will ensure that the retreat can be in both the warm and cooler regions of the cage. This will set up thermal gradients that allow the lizard to select a body temperature that is most comfortable for it. The substrate in the hide area should be checked and cleaned frequently, and after fecal matter is removed, should be replaced if needed.

A branch in the cage may enhance the beauty of the enclosure. Although leopard geckos rarely climb, branches may assist in the shedding process and also allow for additional hiding areas within the enclosure. There are many sources for both natural and artificial branches, including pet stores, online retailers, and herp expos. The advantage of natural branches is they are easily obtained; the disadvantage is that they are difficult to properly sterilize should the need arise. You can gather branches from outdoors, provided you gather only branches from nontoxic species of trees and thoroughly clean and sterilize them before use.

If the keeper decides to use plastic branches, care must be exercised in deciding which brand to use. A lot of the plastic branches available have an access hole in the bottom going inside of the branch. This is a factor related to their manufacture. If left open, there is a possibility that the lizard will go into the hole inside of the branch, making it difficult to retrieve

Adding moss or other moisture-retaining substrate to your geckos' hiding place is a great way to maintain adequate humidity levels.

him. We have seen other species of lizard becoming stuck and suffocating. If you choose to use a plastic branch, a good strategy is to plug the hole to prevent mishaps from occurring.

## Humidity

The easiest way to maintain proper humidity levels in the cage is to use a shallow water dish. Leopard geckos drink on occasion in captivity. They also acquire a lot of the moisture that is needed for their metabolism as preformed water in their diets. Leopard geckos do best if provided with fresh drinking water at least once weekly.

Providing a hiding area containing dampened substrate is perhaps the best way of supplying adequate humidity. We have found this to be useful in aiding the gecko during the shedding process. If some of the shed becomes stuck on his toes, parts of them may become necrotic and fall off. Once the toes have fallen off, the animal never regrows them (unlike the tail).

### Geckos Need Choices

A good strategy is to have a hiding area in the warm region of the cage and another in the cool area of the cage. This allows the animal the option to choose his preferred body temperature and still be able to hide.

# Chapter 3

# Feeding

Leopard geckos are one of the easiest lizards to feed under captive conditions. Indeed, if you have one that is not feeding, it might be a good idea to bring it to a reptile veterinarian, as there may be something wrong with your animal. Leopard geckos are insectivores and will feed upon any appropriately sized insect. In the wild, they have been known to feed on insects and other invertebrates, small mammals, and other lizard species (Puente, 2000).

# Crickets

Most people prefer to feed their captive geckos crickets supplemented with the occasional king mealworm. Crickets can be purchased at most pet stores or at the various reptile shows occurring across the country. Purchasing a few crickets weekly may become expensive. They can be purchased in lots of one thousand to make their use more cost-effective.

A great advantage to keeping a large number of crickets is that you will always have some available for feeding. The downside is that you need to have the proper setup to maintain the crickets until you can use them. Large numbers of crickets can be maintained in medium plastic trashcans. Make sure they cannot escape their enclosure. If they do, crickets can survive in the house for many months feeding on crumbs, cat food, etc., until they perish. Having some sort of screened lid will help prevent escapes. Egg cartons or paper towel rolls inside the enclosure act as resting regions for the crickets.

Crickets need to be maintained at approximately 80°F (26°C) and must have continuous access to food and water. Water can be provided with daily greens (such as collard greens or kale), pieces of carrot, or slices of orange. Do not use water bowls that do not provide a way for the crickets to easily get out of the container; they drown quickly and large numbers will die if they cannot escape the water bowl. A lot of keepers use cotton in the water bowl to prevent this. There is also a product available that provides water in gelatin spheres. Keeping large numbers of crickets can become tedious, especially if you only have one or two geckos.

# Cockroaches

The use of cockroaches as a food item for reptiles and amphibians has been increasing. Cockroaches are an easy-to-breed food item with high nutritional content, if properly fed.

There are several varieties, including the orange-headed cockroach (Eublaberus prosticus), that do exceptionally well with minimal care. The other bonus in keeping orange-headed cockroaches is that they cannot climb glass, which makes rearing them easy. A 10-gallon (38 l) aquarium would make a good cage for this type of cockroach. Some of the other types of cockroaches, like Madagascan hissing cockroaches, need a layer of petroleum jelly around the top inside perimeter of the cage so they cannot escape. Failure to add this layer will make for a very unhappy spouse if cockroaches suddenly appear in large numbers in the house or apartment.

As a cage substrate, use dry heat-treated (200°F/93.3°C for 20 minutes) bran. Heat-treating will kill any eggs of moths or beetles in it. The cockroaches will use a couple of egg cartons as hiding areas. Orange-headed cockroaches give "live birth;" actually, the female retains the eggs in a special pouch in her abdomen. If you start a culture with ten pairs of adults, you should have various sizes from which to choose within several months.

For leopard geckos, cockroaches no larger than three-quarters of an inch (1.9 cm) are adequate for a food item. Like crickets, cockroaches need to be gut-loaded with green leafy lettuce, orange slices, and dry dog food before offering them to your gecko.

Other species of roach are sometimes available as feeder insects. As long as they are not too big or too small, you can offer them to your gecko. Examples of these species are the orange-spotted roach (*Blaptica dubia*) and the death's head roach (*Blaberus cranifer*).

## Mealworms

Mealworms are also easily maintained under captive conditions. A plastic tub with bran or oatmeal works very well as basic housing. The essential ingredient for successfully rearing mealworms is maintaining a lot of food in the enclosure with the mealworms so they grow and do not feed on each other. Also, a source of water is important. We use either damp paper towels placed on top of the substrate or sliced potatoes. Some other great sources of water are slices of oranges and carrots, which will also provide more nutrients to the mealworms before feeding them to the geckos. Change the slices of vegetable or damp paper towels daily to prevent mold growth. Mealworms will breed under these conditions, allowing you to have different sizes of worms readily available.

## Other Choices

Other insect prey can also be supplemented to the basic cricket/mealworm diet, and

## Overfeeding

It is easy to make your leopard gecko obese if you overfeed it. This is, in part, due to the high fat content of some food items. For example, too many mealworms in its diet may lead to medical problems such as obesity or hepatic lipidosis—fatty liver (DeNardo). An obese leopard gecko has a very large, heavy tail and body. Just like in humans, obesity can lead to an early death for your pet, so you should avoid that condition. If in doubt about your leopard gecko's weight, consult a herp veterinarian.

your pet leopard gecko will appreciate the change. These food items include silkworm larvae, tomato hornworm larvae, and the occasional pink (hairless) mouse. A tomato hornworm or large silkworm has many times the calories of a cricket and should thus only be used in moderation. Again, this is to avoid obesity.

There are also several commercially prepared diets available. Some of these include canned crickets and mealworms. The advantage of using such a diet is the ease of maintaining these food items (e.g., you just open the can when you need them). The disadvantage is that the food item is not moving and a lot of leopard geckos need the movement as a cue that there is food in the cage. We have not had much luck using these prepared food items with our leopard geckos, although they are acceptable to other species of lizard such as bearded dragons.

## Feeding

A healthy leopard gecko will need to eat at least four or five appropriately sized crickets per meal. If you also use mealworms, a mealworm in addition to these four or five crickets will be plenty of food for the lizard. For an adult gecko, meals should be fed at least a couple of times weekly. More feedings are necessary for hatchling or juvenile geckos. If you use silkworm larvae or tomato

Mealworms can be set up in a breeding colony very easily.

hornworms, you may want to reduce the number of food items. Feeding a leopard gecko large numbers of these larvae may be problematic in that the possibility of obesity is greatly enhanced.

A skinny leopard gecko will have a very thin tail, and the pelvic girdle will be evident. An animal with these characteristics needs to be fed more frequently. If after frequent feedings he is still skinny, a trip to a veterinarian specializing in reptiles is in order. Each lizard is an individual. The keeper will have to observe his or her animals and see how their weight responds to the feeding regimen. That regimen will then need to be adjusted if the gecko starts to gain or lose too much weight.

Never feed your leopard gecko more than it can eat in one sitting. If that means removing the excess crickets in the gecko's enclosure after a few hours, then that task must be done. Check under any hiding areas, including the water bowl, for any wayward crickets or mealworms.

Leopard geckos are nocturnal animals. Because of this, it is best to feed your pet gecko at night. This prevents mishaps like feeder animals feasting upon it while it is sleeping during the day. A second good feeding is to offer your gecko food in shallow dishes that the prey item has difficulty escaping from. There are several such dishes on the market, and they are reasonably priced. This is especially useful in the naturalistic terrarium. If the cricket or mealworm escapes, it can live on the plants or sleeping lizards for months until it dies. This can ruin foliage used to decorate the terrarium. Another problem with loose food items is that the crickets or mealworms will lose their nutritive value every day that they are not eaten.

## Calcium Supplementation Tip

Calcium can be easily provided to leopard geckos with a shallow dish in one part of the cage. Placing calcium powder and food items that cannot climb out in this dish, such as mealworms, ensures that some of the calcium will adhere to the food before the gecko eats it. Some geckos will lick up the calcium even when no feeder insects are present.

## Gut-Loading

There are a couple of steps that need to be followed *before* crickets or mealworms are fed to your gecko. All food items should be supercharged with good nutrition before they are

You can offer an adult leopard gecko an occasional pinkie mouse if you wish.

offered, which means gut-loading insects and worms with nutrient-rich food beforehand. Commercial cricket diets, chicken food, powder from rodent blocks, and baby cereal flakes make a good basic diet (de Vosjli et al., 2004). Grated carrots, sliced oranges, and dark greens like kale or red-leaf lettuce can be added. This diet will provide the nutrients necessary to encourage your gecko's proper growth and development. A good method is to feed the crickets and mealworms 24 hours before introducing them into the gecko cage. Doing this ensures that they have had time to assimilate the nutrients before the leopard gecko feeds upon them.

## Supplements

The food items also need to have supplemental minerals and vitamins added to them. To accomplish this, place some powdered supplements in a large plastic cup. Put the crickets or mealworms inside of the cup and gently shake the contents so that some of the supplement adheres to them. The supplement will stick to the food items long enough for the gecko to ingest it when he feeds upon them. Crickets will actually retain a lot of the supplement for several hours after having it placed on their exoskeleton. Another strategy is to use shallow food dishes with the supplement on the bottom.

You should use only a reptile-specific vitamin and mineral supplement. Many brands are available at places that sell reptiles and pet supplies. The best vitamin supplements have vitamin A in the form of beta carotene, which will help prevent overdosing your gecko on this nutrient.

Following these steps is vital to ensuring the long-term health of your leopard gecko. Providing supplementation is especially important in preventing metabolic bone disease.

## Water

Even though leopard geckos live in a xeric habitat, they need to have regular access to water. Providing water is easily accomplished by simply placing a shallow dish in the enclosure or naturalistic habitat. All sorts of water dishes work, from a plastic lid to a specially manufactured naturalistic water container. The key is that the water dish must be regularly cleaned and refilled with clean, fresh water. If the water is soiled and not replaced, an

## The Right Way to Prepare Food Items

We have all heard the expression, "You are what you eat!" This simple saying can be applied to leopard geckos as well. Using the proper methodology to prepare food items before presentation to the gecko is key to the long-term survival of your pet. Food preparation can be broken down into two parts: gut-loading and supplementation. Gut-loading involves feeding the cricket, mealworms, silkworm larvae, or other food items a nutritious diet so that necessary nutrients can, in turn, end up in the leopard gecko's gastrointestinal tract.

House the food items in a small plastic cage for 24 hours with no food or water. This ensures the feeder insects will become hungry enough to feed on anything you offer them. Next, offer them greens such as red-leaf lettuce, collared greens, etc. Also, offer chicken food or the powder left over from rodent blocks. These will further enhance the nutritive value of your crickets or mealworms. For moisture, offer orange slices or carrot slices. Allow the crickets, mealworms, etc. to feed for approximately 24 hours before offering them to your leopard gecko.

Before you feed the food items, phase two of food preparation must be implemented—supplement coating. To accomplish this, a 16-ounce (453.6 g) plastic cup is very useful. Place the gut-loaded food items into the cup, and put a small amount of powdered vitamin and mineral supplement in with them. Gently stir the contents of the cup so that the supplement sticks to the food items. Do not use too much supplement. That way, there will be hardly any left on the bottom of the cup when you offer them to your lizard.

unhealthy situation is created. Bacteria and other pathogens are more likely to build up in the fouled water. If the gecko drinks from a dirty dish, the animal may become sick.

Water is also important to ensure that proper humidity levels are maintained in the cage to assist with the shedding process, among other things. Misting the sides of the enclosure is another method used to encourage your gecko to drink. Some keepers even mist the tips of their snouts to encourage drinking.

## Why Isn't My Leopard Gecko Feeding?

A leopard gecko that is not feeding is cause for immediate concern. This condition is often referred to as anorexia. There are numerous reasons a gecko may not be eating, and the cause of this behavior should be explored promptly.

### Dehydration

A very common reason for not feeding is dehydration. If you gently pull back a skin fold and it does not immediately go back to its original position, dehydration is a strong possibility. The first course of action to take for a dehydrated gecko is to add more moisture into the enclosure. If the water bowl is dry, put some clean water in it. Gently place the gecko in the shallow container. Often, the gecko will drink water immediately. If this does not occur, mist some warm—not hot—water on his snout using a spray bottle. Use a gentle spray so as not to startle the animal. Often, the gecko will lick water off of his snout to rehydrate itself.

If, after trying these two strategies, you still have a gecko that is not drinking, fill an eyedropper with water and gently place a few drops into his mouth—give no more that 5 percent of the animal's total body weight in water. You may have to provide water in this fashion for a few days to fully rehydrate it.

Ensure that your pet has a retreat that contains moist substrate. This will allow it to maintain his

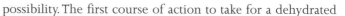

Tomato hornworms are now available commercially and make good feeders for adult leopard geckos.

Many keepers place a small dish of powdered calcium in their leopard gecko enclosure, so the geckos can eat it at will.

water balance more easily, and conditions will more closely approximate those in the wild. Usually, after a dehydrated gecko becomes rehydrated, the feeding response returns.

## Temperature

Another common cause for anorexia in leopard geckos is improper temperature. If the animal is maintained at temperatures that are too cool, he will voluntarily stop eating to prevent food from not being properly digested. On the other hand, if the animal is maintained at temperatures that are too hot, he will also not feed. If the cage rapidly becomes too warm or too hot, the food in the animal's gastrointestinal tract will be regurgitated. It is important to keep the animals in a cage that provides a temperature range from approximately 70°F (21°C) to 88°F (31°C) and have plenty of hiding areas in the enclosure in both warm and cool regions. This will provide the gecko the option of choosing the temperature at which it wants to be. A simple adjustment to cage design can make a world of difference to a non-feeding gecko and will get the animal to feed on his own again.

## Other Problems

If performing all of these adjustments has not helped your leopard gecko to rehydrate, a visit to the veterinarian is in order. The vet can ascertain the animal's condition and explore other possibilities for the poor appetite, including a parasite or protozoan infestation.

# Chapter 4

# Breeding

L eopard geckos are easy to breed under captive conditions. There are many advantages to breeding these interesting lizards, including being able to supply the pet industry with healthy captive-bred individuals, decreasing the demand for wild-caught specimens. In this chapter, we will discuss the basics of leopard gecko breeding, and we will also include a listing of many of the beautiful morphs available.

## Sexing

Central to the successful breeding of leopard geckos is that you have an adult pair. Sexing adult leopard geckos is easy. When they are viewed ventrally, males have enlarged pre-anal pores in the shape of a "V" or a chevron. Also present in males are the bulges from their paired hemipenes, posterior to the vent. To observe the presence of these hemipenal bulges, gently fold the tail over the back of the gecko—be very careful not to break off the tail! When viewed from the side, the bulges are easy to see. Females have very small pre-anal pores, and when the tail is folded over the back, they lack bulges or the bulges are very small. Because leopard geckos exhibit temperature-dependent sex determination, many breeders incubate the eggs at temperatures that allow them to predetermine gender, so often babies of a known gender can be purchased.

## Maturity

Leopard geckos become of breeding age when they attain a mass of approximately 1.2-1.4 ounces (35-40 g) (de Vosjoli et al., 2004; Bergman). This mass usually can be reached between 10 and 24 months of hatching. Healthy, not thin, leopard geckos should be used in breeding projects. In the northern hemisphere, the breeding season for leopard geckos can extend from January to September or October (de Vosjoli et al., 2004).

# Setting Up a Breeding Group

## Cycling

As with most ectotherms, leopard geckos need to undergo a physiological cycling to induce breeding behaviors. Most breeders of leopard geckos accomplish this in two ways. First, the length of daylight is reduced during winter until the heating lights in the enclosure are on only eight hours each day. This change in light simulates conditions that leopard geckos would experience in the wild. During spring, the daylight is increased gradually until lights are on over the enclosure for approximately 14 hours each day. Again, this increase in day length is similar to what leopard geckos would experience in the wild during spring.

The second important cycling consideration is to allow the breeder animals to undergo temperature changes during the course of the year. During winter, enclosure temperatures should be cooler, and during the spring, summer, and fall, enclosure temperatures should be warmer. To heat the enclosures during spring, summer, and fall, a heater is placed underneath the cage at one end. The heaters are connected to a thermostat with the temperature set at approximately 90°F (32.2°C). The background temperature in the room should be cooler. This sets up a thermal gradient from which the geckos can choose their temperature. That is, geckos can maintain their body temperature at the background temperature of the room or to as high as 90°F (32.2°C). As with all ectotherms, this is a more natural condition than simply keeping the reptile room and the enclosure at a constant temperature.

During the winter, the sleeping geckos often use a hiding area. A plastic container with a hole twice the diameter of the gecko's body cut into the side of it will suffice to fulfill this

## To Breed or Not to Breed

Although the current trend in the herp hobby is for hobbyists to breed their animals, you should not feel like a failure if you don't breed your geckos. Not everyone can be a breeder and not everyone should try. You should only attempt to breed your herps if you have carefully considered all that is involved in the project, including what you will do with the hatchlings. Without a plan, you could end up stuck with a large number of lizards to feed and house. Think carefully before jumping into reptile breeding.

## Love Bites

**When leopard geckos mate, the male grasps the female by the neck with his jaws. This can lead to some superficial wounds on the female's neck. As long as they are not deep, bleeding heavily, or infected, you should not worry about them.**

requirement. A substrate of slightly moistened vermiculite will provide extra comfort for the gecko and will help to prevent desiccation during this period of reduced activity. The period of reduced activity and feeding in the winter is called *brumation*.

## Housing

Many successful leopard gecko breeders maintain their colonies in "harem" setups (de Vosjoli et al., 2004; Black, 1997). Ideally, in this setup one adult male is placed with up to five females (Tremper, 2005). To utilize this approach, it is imperative that you have correctly determined the gender of the animals. An extra male could result in an emergency run to the veterinarian to sew up a lizard! We have seen this on more than one occasion. Males combat so violently that occasionally the limbs from one male may end up detached and in the jaws of the other male. Because of the ease of determining gender in this species, this should never occur.

If the harem methodology for breeding leopard geckos is used, make certain that all the females are allowed access to food. Also, make sure that females have access to vitamins and minerals, especially calcium. Occasionally, some females will compete with other females, preventing the latter from feeding. If one female seems to

Many breeders select their stock for unusual and beautiful colors and patterns.

dominate over the others, she may need to be removed from the colony. If only a single pair of leopard geckos is bred under captive conditions, introduce the female into the male's cage.

Leopard geckos are very tolerant of each other if you have a single pair. Because of this, pairs are easily maintained together in one cage. The keeper must be absolutely certain that the two geckos are indeed a pair. If they both turn out to be males, problems are certain to ensue. On the other hand, two females will live peacefully together in the same enclosure.

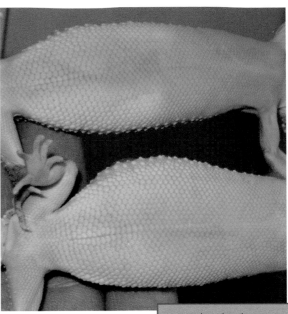

Leopard geckos have translucent abdomens, allowing you to see developing follicles (bottom) and near-term eggs (top) in your females.

## Courtship

If both male and female are ready to breed, the male will copulate readily with the female once she is in his territory. However, females that are not receptive to breeding will demonstrate behaviors indicating this. These behaviors include tail wagging, letting out a distress call, and flattening their bodies in an attempt to make themselves look larger. It probably is prudent to remove the female from the male's enclosure at this time and attempt to induce breeding at a later time. If such behaviors are not observed, let the female remain in the male's enclosure. More often than not, the keeper does not observe breeding. During the mating act, the male usually grasps the female on the neck with his mouth, a behavior known as a copulatory grasp. Actual breeding usually lasts for less than 5 minutes.

## Gestation

If the female leopard gecko becomes gravid (pregnant with eggs), her eggs will soon be visible through her belly due to the translucent nature of her skin. Most often leopard geckos have two eggs at a time, but occasionally they have one. The good news is that

# Egg Binding

Egg binding, or dystocia, seems to be rare in leopard geckos. Most cases can be prevented by providing an adequate nest box in which your female can lay her eggs. If the female does not feel comfortable with the nest box, she may hold on to the eggs too long. This can result in egg retention, with the eggs being too large to be laid by the female or with her reproductive organs being too weak to lay the larger eggs. At this point, a trip to the veterinarian is in order. Usually, he or she will try medication, like oxytocin, to induce egg laying. If that does not work, surgery may be required.

females will produce as many as eight to ten clutches annually. Therefore, if conditions are correct, a lot of baby leopard geckos can be generated from a single female. Obviously, if a more healthy diet is provided to the females during the breeding season, it is more likely that a large number of eggs will be produced. As was mentioned earlier, female leopard geckos also need a constant supply of vitamins and minerals, especially calcium, for proper egg development.

## Nesting Sites

During the breeding season, a nest box placed in the enclosure with the female is a very good idea. The nest box can be a simple plastic container 7.9 in. x 3.9 in. (20 cm x 10 cm). In the side of this container, cut a hole twice the diameter of the female to allow the animal access to the inside of the box. Inside the plastic container there should be some dampened sand, vermiculite, peat moss, or a mixture of these. The substrate should be moistened enough so that it barely clumps together when compressed in your hand.

If the female is not utilizing this nest box, there may be a problem with the eggs. More often than not, if the eggs are fertile, the female will lay them in this nest box. In the harem setup mentioned previously, a larger nest box should be incorporated into the enclosure to accommodate multiple females. Alternatively, you can use multiple nesting boxes.

The nest box can be placed in either the warm or cool section of the cage. If two nesting boxes are used, placement of one on the cool end of the cage and the other on the warm end of the cage will provide the gecko with a choice of where to lay her eggs. Monitoring of the nest box on a warm side of the cage is essential to ensure that moisture levels are properly maintained and that the nest box does not become too hot.

## Incubation Methods and Conditions

Most leopard gecko breeders agree that removing the eggs from the nest box and incubating them in an incubator is the most successful methodology for hatching the eggs. They should be moved from the nesting box as soon as possible and placed on top of the substrate in the incubating container. When the eggs are removed, make sure the orientation of the egg from the nest box is kept the same in the incubation box. This ensures that the delicate vessels of the developing embryo are not disrupted. Fertile eggs are somewhat soft and sticky when laid, but they soon become firm and white in coloration. Infertile eggs usually mold within a few days and should be removed from the incubator promptly.

## Incubation Substrate

The eggs need moisture during their incubation period for proper growth and development. The easiest method for providing this moisture is by using a mixture of vermiculite and water as an incubating material. Many breeders use a perlite and water mixture for incubation with great success. Many sources detail precise levels of water and substrate. A mixture of six-parts mix to four-parts water is recommended by de Vosjoli et al. (2004); other sources (Puente, 2001) recommend a one-part water to one-part mix ratio. To be honest, the ratio itself probably does not matter. If the eggs are healthy, they should hatch as long as they are not allowed to dry out. If the adults are maintained in healthy conditions, the eggs they produce should be healthy. Often, the eggs are "bullet proof" if the lizard keeper has correctly prepared the animals producing the eggs. A mix of vermiculite and water that loosely clumps together is probably adequate.

The incubating material should be placed in a large plastic

Female high orange leopard gecko laying her eggs in vermiculite, one of several acceptable laying media.

container, such as a plastic shoe or sweater box, with a few small air holes drilled in the sides. Incubation of leopard gecko eggs can occur in a simple box placed in a warm region of a room or in an incubator specifically designed for incubating eggs. A temperature range of 75°-95°F (23.9°-35°C) represents the extremes at which leopard gecko eggs can be incubated successfully (Viets, 2004). If the temperature of the incubator is higher or lower than this range, the end result will be the death of the developing embryos.

## An Incubation Tip

It is always best to have the incubator set up before the eggs arrive. This allows you to make sure the temperature is correct before the delicate eggs are inside.

A chicken egg incubator works well because it maintains a constant temperature for egg development. Old refrigerators with heat tapes connected to a pulse proportional thermostat also work very well; these thermostats are available at hardware and home improvement stores. A small heat pad used for heating reptile cages is also adequate as the heat source.

Connect the heater to a pulse proportional thermostat, with the probe located inside the refrigerator. The key is to calibrate the incubator *before* any eggs are placed inside of it. The easiest method for accomplishing this is to use an indoor/outdoor digital thermometer to check the temperatures in the incubator. If everything is functioning properly, the daily temperature fluctuation should be no more than 2°F (-16.7°C). If the room in which the incubator is kept has wildly fluctuating temperatures, then a constant temperature inside the incubator may be difficult to achieve. Keeping the incubator in a basement where temperatures are fairly stable may be the easiest way to overcome this problem.

## TSD

Unlike some more familiar animals, leopard geckos and some other species of reptile do not have genetically determined sex. The sex of a leopard gecko is determined by the temperature at which it incubated in the egg. Maintaining a constant temperature for leopard gecko egg incubation is important in sex determination of the hatchlings. Temperature-dependent sex determination (TSD) has been demonstrated in turtles (Madge, 1985; Crews, 1994; Wibbels and Crews, 1995), crocodilians (Crews, 1994), and lizards, including leopard geckos (Coomber et al., 1997; Viets, 2004; and many other references).

TSD in leopard geckos suggests that higher temperatures (90°-92°F/32.2°-33.3°C) produce more male offspring and lower temperatures (79°-80°F/26.1°-26.6°C) produce mostly female offspring; temperatures in between these extremes produce both genders (Black, 1997, 2003). In Viets' studies (2004), several interesting trends were determined: the duration of incubation varies between 36 days (at 90.5°F/32.2°C) and 107 days (at 75°F/23.9°C). At higher temperatures approaching the lethal maximum (e.g., above 90°F/32.2°C), incubation times lengthen again. Viets (2004) has also shown that gender is determined within the first two weeks of incubation.

The implications of the above information to the leopard gecko breeder are manifold. A breeder of leopard geckos can incubate eggs at different temperatures, one for male offspring and one for female offspring. This will allow the breeder to sell babies of a known gender before any external signs can be observed on the hatchling. Often, it is prudent to have more female offspring on hand than male offspring. Only a single male is needed to breed multiple females. This implies that having a generation of more females may be the approach to take if a large-scale leopard gecko breeding operation is desired. Of course, the cooler the incubating temperatures, the longer the incubation period. This allows time for more things to go wrong during the incubation process.

One of the highly desired leopard gecko morphs is the carrot-tail, so named for the bright orange color on the tail.

# Care of Hatchlings

Raising baby reptiles and amphibians to adulthood can often be a daunting experience. However, leopard geckos are a wonderful species with which to acquaint oneself with the intricacies of captive breeding because of their ease of rearing. Hatchling leopard geckos are quite large when compared to other gecko species and can be reared on some of the more easily acquired food items, such as small crickets or mini-mealworms (*Tenebrio obscurus*). The very small hatchling size of many other gecko species, such as banded geckos (genus *Coleonyx*), makes raising the babies to adult size more problematic, as they will initially require smaller prey items.

It is recommended that hatchling leopard geckos be kept individually to avoid competition between cagemates. This will ensure a maximum growth rate of juveniles and will also help to promote a sterile environment and minimize the spread of infectious agents. If you must keep baby leopard geckos in a group, be sure that you keep only individuals of a similar size together. An animal that is substantially larger than his cagemates will likely dominate smaller individuals. This contributes to health problems in the smaller animals and can lead to the demise of the larger animal.

There are many enclosures that can be used for the purpose of rearing leopard geckos. A standard 10-gallon aquarium (37.9 l) is perhaps the best enclosure for those who enjoy

## The Single Gecko

There are probably a lot of people who want to keep a leopard gecko, but have no intention of breeding them. The easiest way of not breeding leopard geckos is to purchase a lone male. However, if a baby was purchased and it turned out to be a female, problems could arise. Female lizards often develop eggs even in the absence of a male to fertilize those eggs, and these females will need a nesting box to avoid egg binding. There has been some research to indicate that "birth control" is a definite possibility in female leopard geckos. DeNardo and Autumn (2000) successfully reduced egg production in lone female leopard geckos by implanting 5 mg of tamoxifen, an anti-estrogen, in the body cavity. Female leopard geckos implanted with tamoxifen did not develop eggs if they were implanted before egg production had begun for the season. In other words, if egg production had been initiated, tamoxifen was ineffective at stopping it. Once off of this drug, some of the experimental animals developed eggs the following season.

viewing their animals and observing their behavior. For those housing larger groups of leopard geckos, a plastic shoebox, or a similarly sized enclosure, works well for rearing babies. This type of enclosure is readily available at most department stores at a very reasonable cost. Plastic is also less fragile than glass and is easily replaced should it somehow be broken.

While hatchling leopard geckos are tiny, they are relatively hardy.

A substrate of paper toweling works very well in these enclosures. Paper toweling is ideal in that it can be monitored for cleanliness and can be replaced easily upon fouling. Although perhaps more esthetically appealing, there are reports of sand leading to gastrointestinal impaction so it should be avoided, particularly when rearing younger geckos that may not be as adept at catching food items without getting a lot of substrate in their mouths.

It is generally the case that leopard geckos will shed within one week of hatching. As in the case of adult geckos, this first shed is usually ingested, so do not become alarmed if you do not observe shedding behavior.

Following the first shed, baby leopard geckos should be offered two-week old crickets. Within a few weeks, they will be large enough to accept three-week old crickets. As a rule, it is wise to feed several small crickets as opposed to a single large cricket. Smaller prey items allow for easier digestion and minimize the risk of damaging the sensitive gastrointestinal tract of juvenile geckos.

Baby leopard geckos should be fed every second or third day, and uneaten food items should be removed from the enclosure after a few hours. If crickets are left in an enclosure, they will not hesitate to feed on a sleeping gecko. The tail or toes of a leopard gecko make a tasty treat for a starving cricket. All insects must be gut-loaded before being fed to the young lizards. A good vitamin and mineral supplement is also important in ensuring proper growth and development of hatchlings. See Chapter 3 for details on gut-loading and vitamin supplements.

Other food items, for instance mealworms and lobster roaches, should eventually be incorporated into their diet. Do not use

Hatchling patternless leopard geckos. The incubation substrate used here is perlite.

very large mealworms as these are far more difficult for the baby leopard gecko to digest. The ratio of surface area to volume is increased in smaller-sized objects. The larger the surface area to volume, the more readily stomach acids in the gastrointestinal tract of the gecko can break down food. If the food item is too large, the likelihood of digestion is reduced. If the prey is too large, it may be regurgitated by the animal. This is stressful to the lizard and should be avoided at all costs.

Hydration is an important aspect of the captive propagation of reptiles, particularly in the case of juveniles. Water should be provided to hatchling leopard geckos at all times. A milk bottle cap or similarly sized, small, shallow plastic container works very well for this purpose. Misting one side or corner of the enclosure is another way to provide young leopard geckos with water, but avoid misting the entire cage as this can promote bacterial and fungal growth. In addition to providing a more "natural" source of water, misting the enclosure serves to raise the humidity level within the enclosure, which aids in the molting process.

Proper heating is an integral aspect of raising and maintaining reptiles, as they require a heat source for basic metabolic function. Heat should be provided to hatchlings via an undertank heater, such as a heat tape or heat pad. It is very important to connect the heat source to a thermostat and maintain a stable temperature of 30°C (86°F). DeNardo and

Autumn (1995) showed that providing supplemental heat in the leopard gecko enclosure during the day increased the growth rate of the young lizards.

An animal must feel secure in his environment to ensure proper development. This is best accomplished by providing a hiding area where the gecko can escape from view and rest comfortably. This can take a variety of forms, including everything from an artificial rock hut to a paper towel roll. Anything that offers security for the cage resident is helpful for the proper development of the baby leopard gecko.

## The Amazing Leopard Gecko Morphs

With the boom in captive breeding, numerous colors and patterns of leopard geckos that are not found in the wild have recently emerged in the market. These human-produced colors and patterns are called *morphs* by hobbyists. It seems a new morph is generated almost every year.

Currently, there are over 30 different morphs of leopard gecko available, most of which have been developed over the past 8 to 10 years (Tremper, 2005). As with anything, the initial cost of a new color morph can be staggering—up to several thousands of dollars. However, due to the ease of leopard gecko breeding, it usually does not take long before extravagant morphs of gecko become affordable to the general public. This has been evident, especially in the amelanistic morphs that were recently exorbitant and which are now available for less than ten percent of their original price.

Amelanistic (i.e., albino) is one of the most popular of the leopard gecko morphs. This is an amelanistic hatchling.

There are several forms of amelanistic leopard geckos. Two—a light and a dark form—are pictured here.

Leopard gecko morphs have been broken down into variants in pattern and variants in color. A lot of the various morphs are simply designated as "designer morphs." Many are the result of various combinations of pattern and color morphs. It should be pointed out that egg incubation temperatures not only affect the gender of the leopard gecko, they also may have a large effect in determining pigmentation (Viets, 2004). Therefore, some of the morphs offered for sale may be the result of the temperatures at which the eggs were incubated and not a true genetic variant. Make sure that you investigate this with the leopard gecko breeder before making the big purchase.

From the initial stock of wild-caught leopard geckos, captive breeders have generated numerous leopard gecko pattern morphs including: jungle, striped, reverse striped, patternless, and color morphs such as high yellow, white, lavender, ghost, amelanistic, melanistic, leucistic, and others (de Vosjoli, 2004; Tremper, 2005). There is also the "giant" form of leopard gecko that attains a much larger size than average.

## Normal

The typical or normal pattern of a leopard gecko is one that has two dark saddles across the body and three or four tail rings. The body also has numerous dark spots, hence the common name leopard gecko. The head is covered with smaller spots as well. These spots are black, brown, or purple in coloration. When leopard geckos are babies, their body saddles are more evident, but they fade with time as individuals mature. The ground color of the "banded" leopard gecko is a dull yellow or light cream. Nevertheless, these wild-type leopard geckos can be stunningly beautiful in their own right.

## High Yellow

The high yellow variety is an animal that has more yellow coloration than is normally found in leopard geckos. The dark leopard spots are reduced in size, with more yellow background showing through. The result is a brightly colored leopard gecko that is quite appealing to many hobbyists. This was the only variation available to reptile breeders from 1975 to 1990 (Tremper, 2000).

## Jungle and Striped

Just like some of the other popular forms of reptiles, such as the ball python and the carpet python, the leopard gecko has a variant known as the "jungle-phase." As described by Tremper (2004), this form has irregular, asymmetrical, and dark body blotches. The ground color is often sulphur yellow and the tail is nonringed. The stark contrast between the ground color and the blotches gives this animal a striking appearance. According to Tremper (2000), this form was originally produced in 1994 and gave rise to the first fully striped gecko.

Genetic striping is a pattern variant noted in many reptiles, including leopard geckos. The striping in leopard geckos may not be as dramatic as it is in other reptiles, but it is interesting nonetheless. The striping may be complete from the neck to the tail, or only partially extend down the body of the animal. There is even a reversed striped morph that has a dark pigmented vertebral stripe. The tail in both forms may be striped or blotched.

## Patternless

The final patterned morph is the patternless leopard gecko, often mistakenly called the leucistic. As adults, these geckos lack the spotted pattern of normal leopard geckos. Because they lack spots, their bodies take on a unicolor appearance. There are several color variations that are considered to be patternless, and patternless leopard geckos are known to change color dramatically based on mood, lighting, temperature, and other factors. The most

### Keep Good Records

If you want to set up a selective breeding project, keeping detailed records is essential. You will want to keep track of each gecko's parents, siblings, and offspring and the genetics of each. Also, note anything unusual, such as an abnormal growth rate, color change, or other developments. Without careful record keeping, you will be unable to properly pair your geckos to produce the desired appearance in the offspring.

The jungle morph has a broken and irregular pattern and lacks rings on the tail.

desirable ones are creamy yellow in color. Baby patternless animals are pale and spotted with brown or bronze.

## Orange and Tangerine

There are also varieties that exhibit orange and tangerine coloration on part of the body and the base of the tail. The orange is usually anterior to the tail base, and leopard geckos with very orange tail bases are often called carrot-tails. This morph has been crossed with the patternless morph resulting in leopard geckos that are nearly solid orange. According to Tremper (1996), this variety was first produced in 1996.

## Blizzard

The blizzard color morph is a white lizard possessing blackish-blue eyes (Vella, 2000). This morph has a head that is light gray in coloration and has almost a translucent body. The bodies have a slight yellow overcast, and the tails are white. This is different from true leucistic morphs in that they do have a slight pattern, according to Vella (2000). The adults that produced the first blizzard leopard gecko were abnormally large and had heavy speckling. When bred to leucistic leopard geckos, the blizzard morph produced mostly offspring that were normal in coloration and appearance. However, the same cross did produce one bright yellow colored baby that showed characteristics of both the adults. This bright baby was given the name "banana blizzard lizard" by Vella (2000).

## Patternless vs. Leucistic

Patternless leopard geckos are often called leucistic, but these terms actually mean different things. The patternless geckos simply lack the normal leopard gecko pattern. Leucistic animals (geckos, snakes, or other species) have a white pigment overlaying normal color and pattern. Unlike an albino, the eyes of a leucistic are not pink but are usually blue or black.

## Amelanistic

The amelanistic leopard gecko is another popular color morph. These animals contain no melanin in their skin, and the overall coloration is dominated by a beautiful yellow hue. They are often called albinos, although amelanistic is the more accurate term. Many breeders are crossing this morph with some of the other morphs mentioned, which results in an even larger number of color morphs.

The early amelanistic leopard gecko did not have the red eyes typically associated with other amelanistic reptiles and amphibians until 2005, with the R.A.P.T.O.R leopard gecko morph bred by Ron Tremper. The R.A.P.T.O.R. leopard gecko (acronym for ruby-eyed, albino, patternless, Tremper line orange) is a beautiful brightly colored lizard first described in 2005 (Tremper, 2005). This animal was selectively bred from a tangerine patternless albino called A.P.T.O.R. (for albino, patternless, Tremper line orange) gecko (Tremper, 2005).

The hypo tangerine leopard gecko is so named because it is hypomelanistic and bright yellow-orange in color.

If the list of all of these color morphs seems daunting, keep in mind that even a normal banded form has an inherent beauty. Leopard geckos, regardless of their coloration or pattern, make outstanding pets. However, for those with an entrepreneurial outlook on reptile keeping, leopard geckos provide the ideal opportunity to enjoy a rapidly changing and exciting hobby. Whether it is your first reptile purchase, or the hundredth time that you have sworn it will be your last, owning a leopard gecko is guaranteed to provide you with a truly rewarding experience.

# Chapter 5

# Health Care

L eopard geckos are a hardy species, and with proper care they can live for around 20 years. Visits to the veterinarian should be few and far between if the keeper initially selects a healthy animal and practices good husbandry. Health-related issues for leopard geckos will run the gamut from mild to serious problems. Naturally, the goal of the keeper is to prevent any problems from occurring at all.

A lot of the health issues discussed are the result of poor cage design. Carefully review habitat requirements *before* purchasing a leopard gecko to prevent any problems caused by improper care of the animal on your part. If you have other geckos, it is necessary to keep your new gecko quarantined—even if your veterinarian has deemed it healthy.

Establishing a relationship with a reptile veterinarian is important to the long-term health of your gecko. A fat-tailed gecko is pictured.

## Choosing a Veterinarian

A veterinarian with reptile experience is becoming less difficult to find. With the availability of books specific to reptile medicine and Internet information, your veterinarian has much more knowledge available to him or her than in the past. Find someone you trust to handle your animal properly, make a timely diagnosis, and charge prices that you can afford. A good strategy is to take any newly acquired animal in for a health check. Then, if your pet leopard gecko appears ill or even just a little "off," it is nice to have an already established working relationship with a reliable vet. Good veterinary care can mean the difference between your new pet surviving a few months or living for many years.

## Shedding

A leopard gecko sheds his skin occasionally. If the lizard takes on a dull, cloudy appearance, this probably indicates that the shed process is occurring. Skin then peels off the body in pieces, which the gecko usually consumes. It is unknown if this is for the nutrient benefit or to reduce the attraction of predators.

Occasionally, there are problems with shedding, usually when the skin adheres to the toes. More often than not, these problems are related to poor husbandry. If the skin will not peel from the toes or other portions of the body, a soak in warm water may help alleviate the problem, as long as the poor shed is due to a lack of humidity. However, health problems may be at issue, and if that is the case and the skin is firmly attached, moistening the skin with hydrogen peroxide (except around the eyes) may be necessary. To soak your gecko, place it in an escape-proof container with a water level that just reaches its belly. The soak can last as long as an hour or until the water cools. Always supervise a soaking lizard.

To increase humidity for successive sheds, be sure there is a shallow container for water in the enclosure, as well as a hiding area containing moist substrate that the gecko can utilize at will. If your gecko appears ill or continues to have difficulty shedding, a visit to the veterinarian would be advisable. If the toes have been impacted by a bad shed, putting a bit of antibacterial ointment on them to prevent any infection is a good idea.

## Tail Loss

Like many other lizards, leopard geckos can readily lose their tails. Grabbing an animal roughly by the tail will result in a less than perfect specimen. Keeping two male geckos in the same enclosure may result in tail loss due to fighting. Injuries caused by cage furniture or the family cat are also possibilities, and the gecko owner needs to be aware of all these possible predicaments. Tail loss is not the end of the world for the gecko; it will regrow, but will not be as attractive as the original tail. You can dab the site of the break with antibiotic ointment to prevent infection, if you wish.

## Finding a Reptile Vet

It is not always easy to find vets who are experienced with reptiles and amphibians. Here are some suggestions to help you locate a vet who can help with your pet leopard gecko.

- Call veterinarians listed as "exotic" or "reptile" vets in the phonebook. Ask them questions to be sure they are familiar with leopard geckos.
- Ask at your local pet stores, animal shelters, and zoos to see if there is someone they can recommend.
- Call herpetological societies as they are likely to know which local vets treat reptiles and amphibians.
- Contact the Association of Reptilian and Amphibian Veterinarians. Their website is www.arav.org.

## Mouth Rot

Mouth rot gives the mouth a swollen appearance or it may even form scabs around the mouth area. Opening the mouth will reveal scabbed over areas and a purulent discharge. Unsanitary conditions or an injury to the mouth are the leading causes of mouth rot.

Swab the affected area with hydrogen peroxide once or twice a day. The temperature in the cage may need to be increased if it is not optimum. If the gecko has a respiratory infection along with the mouth rot, or if the mouth infection persists for more than a few days, it should be taken to the vet so that the lesions can be swabbed and cultured. Mouth rot can become serious, so you should start treatment immediately.

## Injuries

Fights between geckos kept together in a colony may be the most frequent cause of injuries. Males tend to fight more, but females will also demonstrate dominant and aggressive behavior. Thermal burns, resulting from either touching a heat lamp or another heat source, can result in severe injury, permanent scarring, or even death.

Most injuries require only a topical antibiotic, but in more serious cases, such as deep wounds or burns, a vet will need to be consulted. At least part of the recommended therapy will probably include the use of injectable antibiotics.

Leopard geckos and other eublepharids normally eat their shed skin, although the reasons for this are unclear.

## Respiratory Infections

Respiratory infections are usually the result of keeping an animal too cool. If an animal has a bubbly or mucoid discharge from the mouth, or it gapes, gasps, or wheezes, check the temperature in the cage. Make sure there is a substantial area where your gecko can hide that is around 85°F (29.4° C). If not, your initial effort should be to bring the temperature up to this optimum condition. If there is a cool side that is usually kept at 70°-75°F (21.1°-23.9°C), you should increase that area to around 80°F (26.7°C).

Retained shed skin has constricted the wrist of this leopard gecko. Proper humidity will usually prevent skin retention.

If your animal is not greatly improved after a few days, it will need to be taken to the vet for an examination. At this time, it will also probably be placed on antibiotics.

# Signs of an Unhealthy Gecko

If your gecko displays any of the signs in the list below, it may need veterinary attention. If you are in doubt, it is better to seek the opinion of a veterinarian with experience in reptile medicine than to wait and see what happens. The sooner the animal sees the vet, the greater the chance it will recover.

- abnormal feces—runny, odd color, excessive odor, worms
- inability to right itself when turned upside down
- listless or sluggish behavior—can be caused by cool temperatures
- refusing food—can be caused by temperature extremes
- shedding problems—especially if skin is constricting toes, feet, or limbs
- sunken eyes
- vomiting
- weight loss

## Parasites

All newly acquired leopard geckos should be examined carefully for parasites. A fecal analysis on a fresh stool is fairly inexpensive and can save much in time and expense at a later date. A direct smear as well as a fecal flotation should be analyzed. Fecal analysis can reveal several types of parasitic infection—most commonly, nematodes, trichimonads, amoebas, and coccidia.

Outward signs of a parasitic infestation might include lack of appetite, runny or bloody stools, lethargy, weight loss, and dehydration. Virtually all parasitic infections in leopard geckos are the result of poor husbandry practices. Parasites are transmitted when the feces of an infected animal pollute the food or water of another animal. Therefore, proper personal as well as habitat cleanliness is imperative for raising healthy animals. Hand washing before and after dealing with each gecko is important in preventing transmission of disease.

Cage cleanliness is also extremely important, and stools should be removed on a regular basis. During treatment for parasites, animals should be housed individually in simple enclosures with a paper towel substrate. The toweling should be changed and the cage itself washed frequently, preferably each time the animal defecates. Disinfection of the cage can be accomplished by washing it with a mild soap and bleach solution. This will prevent the animal from becoming re-infected while he is undergoing treatment.

Nematodes are most commonly dealt with by treating the gecko with fenbendazole at a dose of 75 mg orally every seven days for a total of at least three treatments. At this time, the feces should be reevaluated to ensure there are none remaining.

Amebiasis and flagellate protozoans such as trichimonas are both treated with metronidazole orally at a dose of 50 mg every seven days for at least three treatments. A follow-up fecal exam should reveal if any problems remain. If your vet prescribes a different medication or gives different advice, follow your vet's instructions.

This gecko has suffered a bad bite from an aggressive male.

Coccidia are generally associated with an unclean environment and are highly contagious. Therefore, if you introduce an infected animal into another animal's clean environment, you may unwittingly begin a huge problem. The oocysts (eggs) of the coccidian are present in the feces. Bloody stools resulting from hemorrhagic enteritis may be seen with severe infections. Sulfadimethoxine is most commonly used to treat coccidiosis. It is given at a dosage of 50 mg daily or every other day until the animal is feeling better and the stools no longer contain oocysts. With coccidia, it is extremely important to maintain a clean environment during treatment.

## Cryptosporidiosis

One coccidian parasite that probably will not respond to treatment is the insidious *Cryptosporidium*. It can be transmitted to humans, so care should be exercised when handling an infected animal. The use of disposable gloves and effective hand washing should be included when dealing with an animal infected with *Cryptosporidium*. Regurgitation and weight loss may well continue despite excellent cage conditions and treatment. An infected animal may be stabilized using trimethoprim-sulfadiazine orally in conjunction with fluid and electrolyte therapy and nutritional supplementation, but ultimately *Cryptosporidium* infection leads to death.

An animal diagnosed with this parasite should never be placed with another gecko because *Cryptosporidium* cannot presently be eliminated. Hygiene must always be viewed as extremely important when handling an infected animal. With these facts in mind, as well as the cost of caring for an animal with this disease, euthanasia may be recommended.

## Metabolic Bone Disease

Metabolic bone disease (MBD) is the result of low calcium levels in the body and causes such symptoms as shaking and a rubbery lower jaw. Leg and spine fractures may also occur. MBD may simply be the result of poor calcium absorption, in which vitamin D3 plays a role. Dusting the insects being fed to a gecko with a mineral powder containing vitamin D3 (preferably one that does not contain phosphorus) can prevent metabolic bone disease. Additionally, a shallow dish filled with a calcium supplement can be kept in the enclosure. The benefit of this is twofold. First, the gecko will lick the supplement in order to satisfy his calcium requirement. Second, the gecko will avoid a possible intestinal obstruction by not licking his substrate in a search for needed calcium.

This leopard gecko is suffering from cryptosporidiosis, a serious parasitic illness.

# Necropsy

The autopsy of an animal is called a necropsy. As unpleasant as it may be to think about, should your gecko die unexpectedly, it is a good idea to have a vet perform a necropsy. This is especially important if you own other reptiles, as the procedure can detect an illness that could affect your other pets. It is important to refrigerate, but not freeze, the body to prevent decomposition. The sooner you do this after death, the more information the vet is likely to find.

Fast-growing young geckos and egg-bearing adult female geckos should have their food items dusted with a supplement at each feeding, while adult geckos that are not egg-laying should have food items dusted with this supplement once or twice weekly.

If any signs of calcium deficiency are noted, a visit to the veterinarian is in order. He or she will undoubtedly prescribe a calcium supplement based on your animal's weight, possibly along with increased usage of vitamin D3 until the condition is resolved. Unfortunately, metabolic bone disease can result in permanent deformities, especially if untreated for too long. Monitoring an animal daily allows you to notice any changes in behavior or appearance and can be critical to maintaining a healthy pet.

# Chapter 6

# African Fat-Tailed Geckos

## by Julie Bergman

African fat-tailed geckos (*Hemitheconyx caudicinctus*) are thick-bodied terrestrial eublepharine geckos endemic (native) to West Africa. They share many of the same physical features of their leopard gecko relatives who live in Middle-Eastern regions. Some of these features are indicated by the literal translation of their scientific name: "hemi" means "half," "theconyx" means "box claw or nail," and "caudicinctus" means "ring-tail" (de Vosjoli et al., 2004). Additional shared features with leopard geckos include eyes with eyelids, size (males up to 10 inches/25 cm, females up to 8 inches/20cm), longevity ( a lifespan of 15-20 years or more in captivity), sexual dimorphism (males are larger than females), nocturnal active period, and the ability to regenerate tails. Differences from leopard geckos include a thicker body and coloration.

African fat-tailed geckos are popular geckos commonly available as wild-caught and, more currently, as captive-bred individuals with many patterns and colors. Captive-bred geckos are far more desirable than wild-caught individuals, which commonly carry a high

*H. caudicinctus* is called the fat-tailed gecko because the regenerated tail is thick and bulbous. Most wild-caught ones have regenerated tails.

parasite load. Only experienced gecko keepers should attempt to acquire wild-caught African fat-tailed geckos as quarantine and treatment for parasites will likely be necessary. A captive-bred fat-tailed gecko is a good second gecko to "graduate to" after mastering the easier care of the leopard gecko.

## Natural History

Fat-tailed geckos come from the West African regions of Cameroon, Nigeria, Senegal, Togo, Mali, and the Ivory Coast. There they live in semi-arid savannah and in bush lands (Henkel and Schmidt, 2004). During hot periods of the day, they live in moist burrows.

## Description

In nature, H. *caudicinctus* have shades of brown and orange in transverse bands on their bodies. A striped phase also occurs in nature that manifests in a white stripe that begins at the head and goes down to the end of the tail (occurring on top of the banded patterns). This phase is less common in nature than the banded phase. Gecko breeders are creating many "morphs" of color and pattern in African fat-tails. Some of the morphs produced are: albino, amelanistic, leucistic, and piebald (produced by VMS Herp). They are not as varied as the morphs available from leopard gecko breeders. However, as time passes, cutting-edge herpetoculturists will no doubt offer a similar large selection of interesting and affordable morphs to future gecko enthusiasts.

## Captive Care

African fat-tailed geckos are similar in captive care to leopard geckos. Some key differences between the two species are that H. *caudicinctus* likes warmer temperatures and more relative humidity than E. macularius. Another lesser known difference is that H. caudicinctus is not as outward with stress symptoms as E. macularius. The gecko keeper, particularly a novice, would not realize his African fat-tail was stressing from a seemingly normal situation such as handling, which a leopard gecko would tolerate more readily.

## Selecting Your Gecko

When selecting an African fat-tailed gecko, it is important to first obtain a healthy one. Healthy fat-tails should look robust and have bright eyes and color. Do not select a gecko with hip bones showing, shed skin stuck to its body, kinks in the tail or back (signs of metabolic bone disease), a thin appearance, fecal matter sticking to the vent, sunken or runny eyes and mouth, or a lethargic response to stimuli. These are all signs of illness, either separately or in combination. Once you have obtained one or more healthy fat-tailed geckos, you can go about setting up a terrarium in your home, provided the animals are all about the same size (males can be slightly larger) and there is only one male in each terrarium.

Fat-tailed geckos naturally occur in a banded phase and a striped phase, pictured here.

Sexing adult fat-tailed geckos is more difficult than sexing leopard geckos, possibly due to the extra fat they have around the vent and femoral pores as compared to the normally less plump leopard gecko. The method of determining sex is the same as with most geckos: looking for the presence of more pronounced femoral pores and hemipenal bulges in the male and the absence of these indicators in the female. As the novice gains more experience, the task becomes easier. Once you have determined gender, you can begin introductions.

## Housing

Geckos, as a group, are territorial, and the commonplace occurrence of regenerated tails in wild-caught fat-tailed geckos (usually due to fighting or predator evasion) seems to indicate that this gecko is indeed very territorial. It is important to supervise introductions closely for the first month or so. When introducing a female to a male or a

## Touchy Geckos

On average, African fat-tailed geckos are a bit less docile than leopard geckos. They usually will adapt to brief periods of gentle handling, but will often nip at first. Fat-tails are more prone to be stressed by handling, as well.

male harem group, it is best to give her the "advantage" by first sterilizing the terrarium to remove pheromone scents from other female(s) and/or the male, rearranging the cage furniture, and then letting her establish herself in the terrarium for a day or two before introducing the other geckos.

Because African fat-tails lack adhesive lamellae and are terrestrial, terrarium setup does not have to include lids or tops if the enclosure is tall enough (i.e., the gecko cannot get out by standing on hind legs from the floor or terrarium furniture) and indoor predators (i.e., cats) are absent. To create a nice visual display in your home, you can use a glass terrarium containing naturalistic-type materials for substrate, hiding places, and decorations. The first step would be to select the proper size terrarium. For one or two adults, a 10-15 gallon (38-57 l) or bigger terrarium is more than adequate. The more adults you have, the larger the terrarium should be. You can also use 16 quart (18 l) or larger plastic sweater boxes for a minimum of one to two adult fat-tails. On each side of the container, about one-quarter inch (6 mm) from the top, be sure to drill at least two air holes. This will provide adequate ventilation for the gecko(s).

## Temperature

Once you have chosen a terrarium, you need to select a method of heating it that will provide a thermal gradient ranging from warm to cool. African fat-tailed geckos prefer a temperature range of approximately 75°F (24°C) as a nightly low to 90°F (32°C) as a daily maximum. As with most geckos, cooling the enclosure during the winter months approximately 10°F (12°C) from the maximum daily temp—in this case about 80°F (27°C)—is recommended for best

Fat-tailed geckos require warmer and more humid keeping conditions than leopard geckos do.

breeding results. Do not let the temperature drop lower than 68°F (20°C).

You may provide heat by using overhead incandescent lighting (an 8.5 inch/22 cm reflector lamp with a household or reptile bulb), UTHs (under tank heating systems such as heat tape or an adjustable thermostat reptile heating pad), or infrared heat (heat without light). Full-spectrum (UVA and/or UVB) type lighting is not necessary with this nocturnal gecko.

When using incandescent or infrared lighting, make sure the fixture is sturdy and not easily knocked over, because this could cause a fire. Start with a low-wattage bulb like a 25-watt household bulb and work your way up if necessary. If using UTHs, make sure you select a brand with an adjustable thermostat.

Offset your heat source to one side of the terrarium to create a thermal gradient from warm to cool. This way your gecko can choose how warm or cool it would like to be; this is important for his metabolism. A timer is handy to turn lights on at dawn and off at sunset. Before introducing the gecko, monitor temperatures at different times of the day with an accurate measurement device like a mercury-type thermometer or digital thermometer with a probe like those sold at most electronics stores. Make sure maximums and minimums are proper.

## Substrate

There are a number of options of what to put inside your African fat-tail's terrarium. First, choose a substrate. Many successful breeders use different types of substrate, for example: newspaper, paper towels, calci-sand, play sand, cage carpet (available in the pet trade), or orchid bark and spaghnum peat moss together. The author has had success keeping H. caudicinctus on 1-2 inches (2.5-5 cm) of spaghnum peat moss topped with a layer of medium grade orchid bark. Medium grade

## Don't Mix and Match

It is important to note that putting different gecko species together in a terrarium is usually a bad idea, unless it is a proven combination that works well. Many gecko keepers unwisely keep the very territorial fat-tailed gecko with the also territorial leopard gecko. This is not recommended because they live in different environments, with fat-tailed geckos preferring more warmth and humidity than leopard geckos. Also, both species, especially the fat-tailed gecko, may not show outward signs of stress and expire before the keeper notices a problem occurring.

is too large to fit in the gecko's mouth. Any substrate the animal could possibly ingest must be monitored by the owner (gecko stops eating, defecates sand, etc.). However, the combination of sphagnum peat moss and orchid bark helps to provide the moisture African fat-tails need to be comfortable in a captive environment.

## Terrarium Furnishings

Once you have decided on a substrate, the terrarium furniture is next on the list. Provide at least two hiding places, one in the warm part of the terrarium and one in the cool part. If you keep multiple geckos, make sure there is enough room in the hiding places for all of them if they choose to be there. Three or more hiding places are wise if you are keeping three or more geckos. Hiding places should conceal the gecko completely. At least one of the hiding places should be a "humid" hide box with a moist substrate like spaghnum peat moss or vermiculite. The geckos will go in there to rest, shed, and lay eggs in breeding situations.

For hide spots, plastic food containers about 4 inches (10 cm) tall and at least 5 inches (13 cm) in diameter with a top that seals work well. Get a larger container to accommodate multiple geckos. Cut a hole in the top big enough for the gecko to get into the container. Put about 2 inches (5 cm) of moist substrate in it. Check the substrate every two to three days to make sure it is moist enough and replace as needed when feces are found.

For variety, you may also put in some half logs made of wood. You can even use household items like paper towel rolls as hiding places. Many esthetically pleasing, sturdy, and washable terrarium furniture items are available in the pet trade. In addition to these hiding places, you can add some driftwood or other securely mounted objects for the geckos to climb on.

Plants may also be used in the enclosure, either fake (cannot die!) or live succulents like *Aloe vera* in pots work well. Leafy plants should be avoided as the gecko may want to sample them and get unknown complications from that.

# Togetherness

Fat-tails frequently will share hiding places, with several geckos sometimes squeezing together into one hide box. Often, a gecko keeper will lift up the hiding place and find the geckos sitting together in a clump.

## Feeding

Once the terrarium setup is finished and your gecko has been introduced, the feeding regimen can begin. First, put food and water dishes in the enclosure. These dishes should be low enough that the gecko can easily get to the food or water and tall enough to keep food items like mealworms from getting out easily. If you have a female, set up a separate low dish for a calcium supplement. She will take what she needs to keep her bones strong and to produce good viable eggs if a male is present. Again, the pet trade has ceramic dishes that suit these purposes nicely. Make sure the dishes are kept clean and free of fecal matter.

Although they are mostly terrestrial, if given access to a branch or rock, your fat-tail may climb on occasion.

Feeding an African fat-tailed gecko is the same as feeding a leopard gecko. It is best to feed adults a variety of food items. You can provide a regular diet of crickets (*Acheta domestica*), which should be about 90-95 percent of the gecko's head size, mealworms (*Tenebrio molitor*), and superworms (*Zoophobas artratus*). Gut-load food items with commercial cricket diet and/or leafy greens and other vegetables at least 24 hours before feeding. Food items should be supplemented with a proven multivitamin with D3 mixed in. You can use a tall plastic cup when feeding crickets; dust them in the cup, swirl it, then feed to the gecko. Food items like worms of different types can be dusted directly in the food dish.

Occasionally, your gecko may be fed wax worms (*Galleria mellonella*) and pinkie mice (not all will take them). Wax worms are high in fat content, highly addictive, and should only be a snack food.

During the warmer summer months, adults may eat as often as three to four times weekly; they will eat about 10-12 crickets or mealworms or about 5 to 8 superworms. In the winter, feeding is reduced to approximately once a week. It is important to adjust the feeding schedule and amount of food to the needs of the individual gecko. Ideally, there should not be a lot of food left over after an hour or so of feeding. Remaining excess food—more than a food item or two—should be removed. Food items (i.e., insects, worms) cannot get nutrition in the terrarium and may bother or even begin feeding on the gecko if present in large quantities.

Also, part of the feeding routine should include misting the sides of the terrarium, which is important in maintaining the humidity the African fat-tail thrives upon.

## Wax Worms

Because wax worms are high in fat, they should not be a staple item in your gecko's diet. However, they are excellent to feed to underweight geckos to help them gain a few ounces.

## Captive Breeding

African fat-tails are not as easy to breed as leopard geckos. In general, many of the same breeding conditions and techniques used with *E. macularius* will work with *H. caudicinctus*.

As with leopard geckos, weight is a better indicator of readiness to breed than age. Fat-tailed geckos will breed at approximately 1.2-1.4 ounces (35-40 grams) of weight. Breeding season usually starts in spring and continues to the early fall. It is important to feed the geckos as much as they will eat just before and during this period so they can keep up with the physiological stress of breeding. The gecko breeder needs to make sure breeding groups are maintaining weight. If weight is not maintained, the affected individuals should be removed and "rehabbed" separately before considering reintroduction to the breeding group. If all the geckos are losing weight, there is likely a stressor present, either a health issue (likely an internal parasite), overcrowding, or dominance issues (geckos do not always get along).

Males can be housed with females (pairs, trios, and as many as one male to five females at a time work well), or they can be housed separately and put with females for a day or two at a time for a few occasions during the first part of breeding season to ensure fertilization (de Vosjoli et al., 2004).

Amelanistic fat-tail laying her eggs in vermiculite, which can also be used as the incubation medium.

## Egg Laying

Approximately 30 days from mating, two eggs—white, round,

and oblong in shape—are laid. A female laying her first eggs, provided a male was present to fertilize them, will often lay an infertile clutch her first time or two. This is common with all types of gecko. A female may lay from two to seven clutches of eggs per year (de Vosjoli et al., 2004). They are usually laid in the moist hide box, although not always. The gecko keeper should take care that the eggs do not desiccate; this can happen rapidly if they are not buried in a moist substrate.

Male fat-tailed geckos are larger and bulkier than the females.

## Incubation

Eggs should be placed in incubation containers with at least 2 inches of moist substrate and with one-quarter of their tops showing. You can use commercially-available clear plastic containers measuring 6.75 x 2.5 inches (17.2 x 6.2 cm), 48 ounce (1.4 kg) capacity, with small air holes for ventilation. Six African fat-tailed gecko eggs may be placed in this size container. For substrate, you can use moistened vermiculite (about 1:1 vermiculite to water by weight), perlite (about 2:1), and sphagnum peat moss (just moisten a little at a time until you achieve desired humidity).

The relative humidity needed to incubate fat-tailed gecko eggs is 70-80 percent. The use of a hygrometer will help the gecko keeper to find the right amount of moisture for the incubation medium. It is best to err on the dry side at first as eggs can usually be moistened if too dry (starting to dent inward); if eggs have been exposed to too much humidity they usually turn red, get moldy, and die.

## TSD

The African fat-tailed gecko is temperature-sex determined (TSD) as is the leopard gecko. Furthermore, both species are Pattern II TSD, meaning there are two pivotal temperatures for sex determination during incubation: 89.6°F (32°C) is the approximate upper pivotal temperature above which high ratios of females are produced, 86.9°F (30.5°C) is the lower pivotal temperature below which high ratios of females are again produced (Viets et al., 1994). At the temperature range between the two pivotal temperatures, males are produced.

Bragg et al. (2000) found that in controlled conditions fat-tailed geckos preferred nesting sites of 90.32°F (32.4°C) to lay their eggs. At this temperature, a 1:1 ratio of males to females is produced. In the same study, leopard geckos preferred much lower temperatures for their nesting sites, 83.66 °F (28.7°C), which skews the offspring incubated at that temperature to predominately female. Bragg et al. speculate this is likely to ensure the survival of each particular species due to better chances of embryo survival or skewing the sex ratios for environmental and other factors needing more research. The study also illustrates the further differences between the two eublepharine species.

Novice gecko breeders should always start out incubating gecko eggs at the lower or middle end of the temperature range for that species of gecko. It is much more difficult to monitor incubation successfully if higher temperatures are used because conditions can change much more quickly for the worse the higher the temperatures get.

For fat-tailed geckos, the lower end of the temperature range is 82.4.F (28°C). A conservative incubation temperature of 85°F (29.44°C) is recommended by de Vosjoli (2004). At this temperature, mostly females are produced. It is useful to know that even well-known sex-producing incubation temperatures are not always reliable and occasionally the "wrong" sex is produced!

Fat-tail hatchlings are smaller than leopard gecko hatchlings. A normal and an amelanistic hatchling are pictured here.

## Hatchlings

African fat-tailed gecko hatchlings will appear as early as 39.5 days at higher incubation temperatures and as late as 72.5 days at lower end temperatures (de Vosjoli et al., 2004). Once they appear, they are usually not hungry, needing a day or so to digest the nutrients in their stomachs that are left over from the egg. Usually, green feces are passed (which is normal), and then the hatchling gecko is hungry.

Hatchling care is just like adult care, everything is just smaller (terrarium, food, etc.) and feeding occurs more often. Place the hatchling geckos in suitable terrariums such as 5-10 gallons (19.9-37.9 l) or plastic shoebox-type setups (just like the adults use). Hatchlings optimally may be raised by themselves or with a clutchmate. Some breeders raise them in small groups. Make sure hatchlings that are kept together are very close to the same size; if one becomes bigger, separate it immediately.

For simplicity, paper towels or newspaper may be used as substrate. You can also use paper towel or toilet paper rolls cut in half as hides. Do not set up a moist hide box because hatchlings are curious and may ingest the substrate. Instead, mist the sides of the terrarium at least once daily in addition to providing a suitable small water dish. Feeding fat-tails is the same as feeding hatchling leopard geckos, provide two-week-old crickets or young mealworms to start; feed daily. Be sure no food is left over in the terrarium as feeder insects, etc., may irritate or attack the young geckos.

## Health Concerns

Medical concerns for African fat-tailed geckos are essentially the same as for leopard geckos (see chapter on leopard gecko health). Imported animals often harbor flagellate protozoans (de Vosojoli et al., 2004). If you decide to obtain an imported specimen, a period of acclimation and quarantine is necessary. You should also consider a fecal exam by a reptile veterinarian if any signs of illness are present or if you are planning to introduce this gecko to your long-term captive geckos. Be sure to set up the terrarium so it is easy to clean in order to reduce the amount of fecal material present; this will better enable you to deal with parasites and bacteria.

Selective breeding of fat-tails is still in its infancy. The most widely available morph is the amelanistic.

# Chapter 7

# Banded Geckos

**B**anded geckos (genus *Coleonyx*) are
eublepharine geckos found in the new
world. They are similar in many ways to the
leopard gecko, only on a smaller scale. Most
banded geckos average only 4-5 inches
(10-12.8 cm) in total length, including the tail.
Because of their smaller size, banded geckos are
more delicate than leopard geckos. Tail loss is
more prevalent in this species, and as a result, they
probably should not be handled like leopard
geckos. As with leopard geckos, banded geckos
possess movable eyelids and lack lamellae on their
feet. They also squeal in displeasure if they are
captured in the field or handled roughly in
captivity. In general, banded geckos do very well
in captivity.

# Natural History

## US Species

The banded geckos found in the US are for the most part desert-dwelling species. The western banded gecko (*C. variegatus*) ranges from southern California, to the tip of Baja California, eastward through southern Nevada, Arizona, Utah, New Mexico, and southward into southern Sinaloa, Mexico (Stebbins, 2003). This form ranges up to elevations of 5000 feet (1524 m). The Texas banded gecko (*C. brevis*) is found in New Mexico, Western Texas, and south into Mexico (Stebbins, 2003). They are found in rocky regions in both desert and woodland regions. The barefoot gecko (*C. switaki*) is found in southern California and Baja California, and frequents low, flat regions up to arid hillsides with rocky boulders. This species is protected in both California and Mexico and cannot

Switak's barefoot gecko (bottom) and the reticulated gecko (top) are the banded geckos that are legally protected and unavailable in the pet trade.

be kept without proper documentation. The reticulated banded gecko (C. reticulatus) is one of the larger species of New World eublepharine geckos reaching lengths of 6.75 inches (17.1 cm). This gecko differs from the Texas banded gecko and the western banded gecko in that it has tubercles scattered over the dorsal surface. The dorsal pattern is also reticulated, hence the specific name. They are found in the Big Bend region of Texas into northern Mexico (Conant and Collins, 1998). The reticulated gecko is protected in both Texas and Mexico, and a scientific permit is required to collect one.

For the most part, the species found in the US are nocturnal animals. Most of the North American species, with the exception of the barefoot gecko (C. switaki) and the reticulated gecko (C. reticulatus), are commonly found during spring and summer. In those seasons, banded geckos are commonly observed on roadways at night. Under optimal conditions, up to 15 specimens can be spotted during the period shortly after sunset until 11:00 pm. They are often seen basking on the road, but, unfortunately, this behavior results in animals being run over on occasion. Even in winter, banded geckos can sometimes be discovered if you carefully examine rock piles.

In the wild, western banded geckos are predators feeding on appropriately sized spiders, solpugids, grasshoppers, beetles, termites, insect larvae, millipedes, centipedes, and isopods (Stebbins, 2003). Texas banded geckos have been observed feeding on moths during a summer nighttime hike near Sanderson, Texas. The moths were attracted to our headlights that shone on

# Some Thoughts for Gecko Hunters

If you decide you want to observe these geckos in their natural environs, always check state regulations to understand the laws regarding search and collection of these animals. In California, a valid fishing license is required for legal collection of these animals; in Arizona and Texas, a valid hunting license is needed. In some states, such as Utah, the subspecies of the western banded gecko are protected and cannot be collected without permit.

If you are looking under rocks, always replace the rock precisely as you found it. This will ensure that the rock can continue to be used as a refuge by animals. Pairs of western banded geckos have been observed under the same rock in mid-March in northern Arizona. These animals were under thin rocks in the sun taking advantage of their warmth and yet remaining hidden from view.

The Texas banded gecko ranges from southwestern Texas to New Mexico and Mexico.

the geckos being observed. Scats from recently collected Texas banded geckos contained remains of beetles. Banded geckos often approach their prey waving their tails back and forth before pouncing on the food item, not unlike a cat!

## Central American Species

Banded geckos are also found in tropical Central America. The elegant banded gecko, (C. *elegans*) is found in southern Mexico, northern Guatemala, and Belize (Bartlett, 1996). The southernmost species, the Central American banded gecko (C. *mitratus*), ranges from Guatemala through Costa Rica (Hiduke and Gaines, 1997). Both forms are found in tropical forests and can be locally abundant (Kruse, personal communication).

On occasion, both the elegant banded gecko and the Central American banded gecko are legally imported for sale in the US. There are also several breeders in the US working with these two species. Always purchase legal animals to avoid difficulties with law enforcement. If you are offered obviously wild-collected animals at a reptile show, it would be prudent to walk away. Captive-bred banded geckos would probably have complete tails and their bodies would not have scars that may have been acquired in the wild.

## Captive Care

### Housing

Banded geckos generally do well in a 5-10 gallon (18.9-37.9 l) terrarium with sand as a substrate. In a 10-gallon (38 l) terrarium, up to four animals (1 male; 3 females) can be safely maintained. A good screen top is insurance against the family dog or cat getting into the cage and making a snack out of your pet.

Captive banded geckos will appreciate a small hiding area, or retreat, to keep them out of human view. This will also help with their sleep cycle, as they are nocturnal animals. As with leopard geckos, cage furniture such as rocks and small branches will make the enclosure more attractive, but are not really necessary for the well-being of the banded gecko.

The use of a red light during the night will allow for observation of your banded geckos during their nocturnal forays. This light should not stress the animals as long as it is on a timer that shuts off in time for the cage to cool during the night. Daytime lighting is not necessary unless plants are maintained in the cage.

Even though banded geckos are a desert-dwelling species, they do not require extremely high temperatures for proper maintenance under captive conditions. In fact, temperatures in the upper 70s and low 80s (about 25° to 28.3°C) work very well with most banded geckos. Keeping a small region of the cage damp will ensure that these lizards will molt their skin properly. This moist area is easily achieved by misting one side of the enclosure several times weekly.

## Natural Environment

Because of their small size, *Coleonyx* are excellent subjects for a naturalistic vivarium. Chapter 2 has information on creating a naturalistic enclosure for leopard geckos, and the ideas presented there can easily be adapted for banded geckos. The US species will do well in a desert-type setup, while the Central American ones will do better in a more humid habitat.

Western banded geckos and the other native US species will fare well when housed on a sand substrate.

If you are keeping plants, a full-spectrum light ensures their proper growth. You will need to provide water to the plants on occasion. This is also useful for maintaining appropriate humidity levels for the health of the banded gecko. Even though they reside in some very arid regions, they should have some degree of humidity in their enclosure. In the wild, these animals spend a lot of time in burrows or under surface debris where humidity can reach high levels.

**Substrate** Substrate choice for banded geckos depends upon the species with which one is working. The more arid-dwelling species like the western banded gecko and the Texas banded gecko will do well on a substrate of sand. The more tropical species such as the Central American banded gecko and the elegant banded gecko require a substrate that retains a little moisture. A mixture of sand and coconut fiber is perfect for this type of substrate. Coconut fiber is available under several product names. Mix the sand and fiber together in a one-to-one ratio. Add just enough water so the mixture clumps slightly in the hand. Add the mixture to the cage. Once laid out, the mixture becomes fairly dry on the top. Moisture percolates up from the bottom of the mixture maintaining proper humidity levels in the cage. Several times weekly, add moisture to the enclosure on one side with a spray bottle. As an added insurance for maintenance of proper humidity levels in the cages for tropical species of banded gecko, adding moist moss on one side of the enclosure works very well.

# Native Plants

When setting up a naturalistic terrarium for banded geckos, you might consider duplicating the habitat by using plants native to the deserts of North and Central America. Several species will fare well in the terrarium. The list below contains a few hardy and available types.

- Copal *(Bursera hindisiana, other Bursera can work, also)*
- Lava fig *(Ficus petiolaris)*
- Ponytail palm *(Beaucarnea recurvata)*
- Rock fig *(Ficus palmeri)*
- Smallflower century plant *(Agave parviflora)*
- Texas tuberose *(Agave maculosa)*

**Hiding Areas** A hiding area will be utilized by these animals and will help ensure a proper feeding response. This area can be a simple plastic container with some damp substrate on the inside. A hole twice the diameter of the lizard is cut through the side of the container to allow access by the animal into the retreat. Check the substrate in the retreat often to remove any feces and to check for uneaten food items. If you want something more natural-looking, there are faux caves and cork bark hollows available at pet stores.

A female Central American banded gecko is emerging from her hiding place in this naturalistic terrarium.

## Feeding

Banded geckos feed on a variety of food items in captivity. A staple of gut-loaded crickets works well with these lizards. The authors kept an adult Texas banded gecko for eight years on a diet of appropriately sized crickets. That was all the gecko would eat, but it never languished until the last few months before its death. As with any insectivore, the food item is only as good as what the food item itself is feeding upon. Gut-loading crickets with various vegetables and fruits such as collards, oranges, dandelions, and prickly pear cactus, in addition to a commercial dry cricket diet, will provide them with good nutrition, which they can in turn provide to your banded gecko. Banded geckos can also be fed other appropriately sized insects.

Feed the adult banded geckos three or four times per week. *Always* remove uneaten food from the enclosure. This may mean checking various areas of the cage, such as under the hiding area, to ensure all uneaten food is found and removed. If left unattended, loose crickets may take a bite out of your gecko while it is sleeping. After awhile, you get a good idea of the number of crickets your gecko will eat per feeding.

## No TSD Here

Because of their smaller size, banded geckos require food items that are smaller in comparison to the food items that leopard geckos feed upon. One- to two-week-old crickets are a good size of food to offer banded geckos. These lizards should have no difficulties engulfing prey items that are this size. Food items in general should be no larger than the width of the head of the banded gecko.

## Captive Breeding

Banded geckos are easy to breed under captive conditions. The problem is raising the neonates because of their small size. Male banded geckos have small spurs on either side of the vent. In females, these spurs are absent. The presence of enlarged femoral pores in males is also a good indicator of their gender. It is important to make sure that you have a proper pair of banded geckos before placing the two animals together in the enclosure. If two males are placed together, the animals may combat each other and inflict damage such as torn off tails and open wounds.

## Cooling

As with most temperate ectotherms, a period of winter cooling, or brumation, is required for successful captive propagation, especially with the banded geckos found in the US. During the fall, slowly reduce

Elegant banded geckos are captive bred in small numbers and remain uncommon in the hobby.

the amount of heat in the banded gecko's enclosure. At this time, do not feed the lizard. This is to allow the gastrointestinal tract to completely digest and void any food before the winter cooling period. Failure to allow for this endangers the lizard. Food that remains in the gut when it is cooled will not digest; and the end result is rotting food in the gut. The lizard may succumb from this. Providing your gecko with a heated enclosure for two weeks before brumation will prevent this problem, as long as you do not feed it any more food.

Note the small spurs near the vent of this western banded gecko; they indicate the individual is a male.

The actual cooling period can last from as little as one month to as long as several months. Monitor the lizards during this period to ensure they do not become too desiccated. Always have a shallow water bowl in with the animals during brumation. The lizards will often move about in their enclosure, albeit very slowly. This is no cause for concern. Much time will be spent in the hiding area as well.

During the spring emergence, turn on the cage heaters. The geckos should start voluntarily feeding within a few days. It is very important to feed females a lot of food so that they can build up sufficient energy stores for egg production. Most banded geckos will lay several clutches of two eggs during their May to September breeding season. Our Texas banded geckos consistently laid two clutches during the late spring and early summer.

# Be Careful

Use extreme care when handling banded gecko eggs. They are very tiny and delicate. You may want to use a small measuring spoon or other tool to move them, rather than your hands.

## Gestation and Incubation

Checking the underbellies of females is a good strategy to ascertain breeding state. The developing eggs are clearly visible on either side of the lower abdomen of a gravid banded gecko. At this time, it is prudent to place a nest box in with the animal. A small delicatessen cup with a hole in it twice the diameter of the lizard makes a good nesting box. As a substrate, use moistened sand, vermiculite, or a sand and

The eggs of Texas banded geckos and other *Coleonyx* can be incubated much like leopard gecko eggs—in warm, humid conditions on a suitable substrate.

vermiculite combination. This will allow the female to lay her eggs in a situation where they will not dry out.

Remove the eggs from the nest box and incubate them in an incubator, if possible. The substrate in the incubation box should be dampened vermiculite: one part vermiculite to one part water by weight. Incubation times range from 4 to 11.5 weeks (Bertoni, 1995). If the eggs are incubated at warmer temperatures, then the length of incubation times decreases. We have successfully incubated eggs from Texas banded geckos and western banded geckos at approximately 82°F (28 °C). C. *elegans* and C. *mitratus* will incubate successfully at 80°F (26.7°C).

## Hatchlings

Baby banded geckos are extremely small and very cute! Because of their small size, they are delicate. Care must be exercised in handling these animals. The use of a small fish net may be beneficial in capturing the baby banded geckos to move them about during cage cleaning, etc. Baby banded geckos are prone to desiccation, so care should be exercised to prevent this. The use of damp paper towels on one end as a part of the cage substrate is a good strategy to prevent this.

Another concern in raising baby banded geckos to adulthood is providing a food item small enough for them to ingest. Neonates will have problems ingesting a lot of the more common food items such as mealworms or large crickets. The best food items seem to be pinhead crickets, newly hatched silkworm larvae, small termites, or mini-mealworms (*Tribolium confusum*). The latter are larva of the confused flour beetle and are a perfect size for baby banded geckos.

The food items should be gut-loaded with greens, orange slices, and dry cricket food. Allow the prey items to dine on these foods for at least 24 hours before giving them to your gecko. Dust them with a good vitamin and mineral supplement before offering them. As mentioned before, never leave uneaten food items in with your baby banded gecko. We learned this the hard way when a few uneaten pinhead crickets started to feed upon a weakened baby banded gecko. The gecko was rescued, but not before damage was done. The crickets chewed on the tail and several toes, and the baby gecko eventually succumbed to the wounds.

A second and third breeding of banded geckos is a possibility if the female receives enough food to replace the energy lost during egg production. Feeding the female gut-loaded food items with adequate supplementation is a good method to ensure her energy stores are quickly replenished. Second clutches usually follow the first clutch 4-6 weeks later. After the second clutch, continue to feed the gecko a lot of nutritious food items so she can regain her strength and weight.

## Health Concerns

Diseases in banded geckos are similar to those of leopard geckos. Nematode worms have been mentioned elsewhere (Bertoni, 1995). The use of fenbendazole at a dose of 75 mg per kilogram for seven days is probably the safest method to treat banded geckos for these internal parasites.

# Food for Hatchlings

Because hatchling banded geckos are so tiny, they can be difficult to feed. If you want to breed your *Coleonyx*, you would be wise to line up sources of tiny insects before the eggs hatch. Below is a quick list of possible food items. Pet stores do not usually carry most of these insects, but you should be able to find a supplier of one or more species on the Internet.

- flightless fruit flies
- flour beetle larvae
- hatchling silkworms
- pinhead crickets
- roach nymphs
- termites

As with many other eublepharids, the pattern of hatchling banded geckos differs from that of the adult. A hatchling *C. brevis* is pictured.

Other problems are generally related to faulty cage design and poor husbandry. Reviewing the information on cage design in this chapter and then remedying in this area may ameliorate these problems.

# Chapter 8

# Goniurosaurus

## by Julie Bergman

One's imagination conjures up all kinds of descriptors for this beautiful Far Eastern eublepharid genus: elegant, colorful, graceful, feisty, and most of all, cool! Indeed, *Goniurosaurus* are sought-after geckos for a reason. Even diehard snake owners are known to have them in their collections. The author recalls keeping some species of *Goniurosaurus* in the 1990s. Gecko aficionados knew so little about them at the time that they were called "purple and brown gonis" for the respective species *Goniurosaurus luii* and *Goniurosaurus araneus*. Thanks to the efforts of an international group of eublepharid researchers and herpetologists, most notably L. Lee Grismer, our knowledge base of this fascinating genus has greatly increased since the 1990s.

# Many Names

The species of *Goniurosaurus* are referred to by several different names in the hobby. They are often called Japanese, Chinese, or Vietnamese leopard geckos. Probably the most common name for them is cave geckos. Many hobbyists call them gonis, a term derived from the scientific name.

Unfortunately, the increased knowledge of *Goniurosaurus* has led to over-collection of this gecko for sale in the pet trade. Grismer was alarmed that *G. luii* was extirpated from its locale by commercial collectors even before his paper came out describing this particular species (Grismer et al., 1999). Over-collection has decimated several populations in many regions of the Far East, and as a consequence, availability of imported *Goniurosaurus* in the pet trade has greatly decreased. Many local governments are now wisely protecting this species. For this reason, aspiring *Goniurosaurus* keepers should seek out captive-bred specimens sometimes available in the gecko trade.

## Natural History

*Goniurosaurus* has been described in three taxonomic groups, the Luii, Lichtenfelderi, and Kuroiwae groups (Grismer et al., 1999). These slender terrestrial eublepharids have movable eyelids and thin toes with claws. Their claws are used to climb rocks and rock faces in mountainous primary and secondary tropical forest environments. During the day they hide inside rock crevices; at night they are active, especially during rain. Their climate is humid.

*G. araneus* is often sold under the names "Vietnamese leopard gecko" and "Vietnamese cave gecko."

## Description

The coloration and patterns of the *Goniurosaurus* are as exotic as their environments, ranging from bright pink to bright yellow transverse bands, and sometimes stripes contrasting with blues to chocolate browns as background. Their tails regenerate, although not with the original concentric bands but interesting irregular patterns. To top it all off, their eyes have different colored irises between species, from blood red to gold.

## The Luii Group

The Luii group contains the most ancient forms of this gecko and is made up of three species: G. luii from southern China, G. araneus from northern Vietnam, and the most recently described species, G. bawanglingensis (Grismer et al., 2002) from the Hainan Island in China. The species in this group are the largest of all the Goniurosaurus with a maximum total length of about 9 inches (230 mm) in G. luii (Henkel and Schmidt, 2004), followed by G. araneus at 7.5 inches (190 mm; EMBL database, Internet) and G. bawanglingensis at under 4.2 inches (107mm) SVL (snout-vent length). Grismer notes that G. bawanglingensis, a gecko protected by limited access to the nature preserve it lives in, has a more robust body than the other Goniurosaurus in the Luii group. G. luii also lives on Hainan Island; however, Grismer believes this form is likely another species with defining characteristics separating it from the form endemic to southern China.

The Luii group also contains the common names gecko keepers are familiar with, such as "Chinese leopard gecko," used for describing G. luii, and "Vietnamese leopard gecko," used for describing G. araneus. Grismer et al. (2002) suggest "Bawangling leopard gecko" for G. bawanglingensis, which is named after the town and nature preserve where this gecko lives. These common names are somewhat misleading as their environments are drastically different from that of leopard geckos, which are from the semi-arid Middle East, and the latter Goniurosaurus , which are from very humid and green Asiatic mountain ranges. Any confusion of the two types of gecko should be avoided as this will lead to mistakes in captive care. G. luii was named for a dedicated individual, Mr. Wai Lui who "spent six years tracking this gecko from mainland China to Hainan Island" (Grismer et al., 1999). G. araneus, which means "spider" in Latin, earned its name from several features it shares with that invertebrate.

## Not for Beginners

Although *Goniurosaurus* are interesting, beautiful, and desirable geckos, they are a poor choice for most beginning gecko hobbyists. *Goniurosaurus* are best suited for advanced gecko keepers because of their difficult requirements in captivity and because it is difficult to acclimate unhealthy wild-caught specimens.

## The Lichtenfelderi Group

The Lichtenfelderi group contains two species, *G. lichtenfelderi* and *G. hainanensis*. *G. lichtenfelderi* are endemic to the Norway Islands offshore from Vietnam. At one time, a population of this gecko found in northeastern Vietnam was thought to be a new species called *G. murphyi* (Orlov and Darevsky, 1999); however, Grismer (2000) demonstrated this gecko was indeed an isolated population of *G. lichtenfelderi*. This species has thin bright yellow bands that sharply contrast with its dark background color and is about 6.5 inches (165 mm) in total length (Henkel and Schmidt, 2004). *G. lichtenfelderi* lives in lowland forests, can be locally abundant, and is associated with the presence of limestone rock (Grismer, 2002).

*G. hainanensis* is found in a bright yellow-banded highland form and a duller-banded lowland form living in mountains along the southeastern edge of Hainan Island. This elusive eublepharid occurs mostly in lower parts of cloud forests and is usually associated with areas containing granite rock (Grismer, 2002). It is a bit smaller than *G. lichtenfelderi*, measuring about 6.3 inches (160 mm) total length (Henkel and Schmidt, 2004).

## The Kuroiwae Group

The Kuroiwae group is known collectively as "Japanese leopard geckos" and lives on the islands of the northern Ryukyu Archipelago of Japan. The Japanese people call them "tokage modoki," which, loosely translated, means "false lizard," or "lizard that is not a lizard." All Kuroiwae group species are designated as national monuments and are protected by the laws of their respective Japanese prefecture governments; *G. yamashinae*, *G. orientalis*, *G. kuroiwae*, *G. toyamai* by the Okinawa prefecture government and *G. splendens* by the Kagoshima prefecture government (Hidetoshi Ota, pers. comm.). These eublepharids are so beautiful and fascinating that when

It is difficult to tell the different species of the Kuroiwae group apart. Some species were formerly considered subspecies of *G. kuroiwae*.

articles about their local ecology or photographs of them appear, damage to local populations results from illegal collection (Grismer, 2002).

The species in the Kuroiwae group are small relative to the

G. splendens is native to the northernmost island of the Ryukyus, Tokunoshima, where it lives in the mountainous interior.

other *Goniurosaurus*; their total length averages from 5.5-6.7 inches (140-170 mm; Kaverkin, 1999). They are often found living on or near limestone, although not exclusively (Grismer, 2002). Although terrestrial, they are also known to run up trees. All have blood red irises, except G. *yamashinae*, which has gold irises. Their background color is generally dark chocolate brown with different colored stripes, spots, bands, rings, and blotches, with many variations of these patterns on the back. Each species has a particular accent color to fill these spots, rings, and blotches.

G. *yamashinae* is the most ancient of the Kuroiwae group (Grismer, 2002) and is endemic to the island of Kumejima. This gecko's Japanese common name is "kume tokage modoki" after the island of Kumejima (Kaverkin, 1999). This form is known to have a pink accent color.

G. *orientalis* lives on the Akajema, Iejima, Tokashikijima, and Tonakijima islands west of Okinawa (Kaverkin, 1999). The Japanese common name is "madara tokage modoki," meaning "blotched false lizard." There is enough variation between the different populations that Grismer (2002) believes there may be other species present. The accent color is orange.

G. *kuroiwae* lives on the main island of Okinawa, and also on two offshore islands (Grismer, 2000). There is lots of variation between specimens because of their wide geographical distribution. The Japanese common name is "Kuroiwae tokage modoki," meaning "Kuroiwae's false lizard" (Goris and Maeda, 2004). The accent colors are various shades of pink.

G. *toyamai* lives on the northern island of Iheyajima (Grismer, 200d). This *Goniurosaurus* has unique features: a robust body and unique broad transverse dorsal bands. The accent color is orange. The Japanese common name is "Iheya tokage modoki," meaning "Iheya's false lizard" (Goris and Maeda, 2004). This eublepharid has "critically endangered" status on the Japanese Red List of Threatened Reptiles (Internet, 2005).

## Look, Don't Touch

**Goniusosaurus are delicate geckos that are prone to stress in captivity. Therefore, handling them should be kept to a bare minimum. These species should only be handled when necessary for enclosure maintenance and to check health status.**

G. *splendens* is endemic to the deep interior of the most northern island of the Ryukyu Archipelago, Tokunoshima (Grismer, 2002). The accent color is bright pink. The Japanese common name is "obi tokage modoki," meaning "banded false lizard" (Goris and Maeda, 2004). This beautiful gecko has been smuggled in large numbers from its native land.

## Captive Care

Goniurosaurus are highly desirable geckos and are sought after by gecko enthusiasts all over the world. As with many exotic and hard to find eublepharids, such as cat geckos (*A. felinus* ), African-clawed geckos (*H. africanus*), and Yucutan banded geckos (*C. elegans*), Goniurosaurus are not often available captive bred, and wild-caught specimens usually carry high parasite loads. Goniurosaurus are best suited for advanced gecko keepers because of their difficult requirements in captivity and because it is difficult to acclimate unhealthy wild-caught specimens.

Goniurosaurus have a shy disposition. In the wild, they quickly run away from humans, and when caught, they emit typical eublepharid squeaky vocalizations (Kaverkin, 1999). As a consequence, Goniurosaurus should only be handled when necessary. Those that may desire to handle their animals should be directed to a eublepharid that tolerates handling well, like the leopard gecko (*E. macularius*). Additionally, shy captive geckos like Goniurosaurus should never be kept with any other type of gecko or living creature.

### Housing

The captive care of Goniurosaurus is similar to that of *A. felinus* in that Goniurosaurus thrive in humid conditions. This is an important factor when choosing a terrarium. Those keeping Goniurosaurus in captivity have had success with both glass and plastic terrariums such as sweater boxes similar in size to the ones used for leopard geckos (see Chapter 2). For the best visual display, a 10-15 gallon (37.9-56.8 l) or bigger "long" style terrarium works well for a pair. It is best for the lid to be partially covered in order to retain humidity as much as possible.

Goniurosaurus should be kept in sexual pairs or similar-sized female-female pairs because there is little known about how groups work in this species. In most other eublepharids, males will fight with each other, so it's best to be cautious and house male gonis separately. Females are usually slightly bigger than males, so a slight size difference in a male-female pair is acceptable.

**Humidity** Humidity-retaining substrates and live tropical plants help create the moist conditions *Goniurosaurus* need in captivity. Spaghnum peat moss is a key humidity-providing ingredient and is used by most *Goniurosaurus* keepers in combination with other substrates. For example, Emberton and colleagues at the East Bay Viviarum in Berkeley (pers. comm.) use sphagnum peat moss mixed with one-third to two-third parts sand, which is again topped with sphagnum peat moss. Kaverkin (1999) used a mix of sphagnum peat moss and bark for his captive breeding project of *G. splendens* at the Moscow Zoo in Russia. Use medium grade orchid bark to help *Goniurosaurus* avoid ingesting substrate while striking at prey items.

A hygrometer (humidity measuring gauge) placed inside the terrarium can be used to measure relative humidity, which should be 70-80 percent. Misting once or twice a day is necessary to maintain moist conditions. At least one misting cycle should occur at night when the gecko is active. Having a misting system automates this task.

All of the *Goniurosaurus* require humid keeping conditions. *G. luii* is pictured.

**Terrarium Furnishings** Once substrate has been established in the terrarium, "furniture" can be selected. Cork bark tubes have been used with success by the author and Kaverkin (1999). They provide a secure hiding place for the gecko and also an area to climb when placed diagonally in the enclosure. Although they are primarily terrestrial, some *Goniurosaurus*, such as *G. orientalis*, are known to climb up trees (Werner et al., 2002), so it is good to give them options— at least until they let you know their preferences by exhibiting

climbing behavior or not. Kaverkin placed his cork bark tubes in both the warm and cool ends of the terrarium, as the keeper should with any type of hiding place in order to provide the animals an opportunity to thermoregulate.

At least one of the hiding places should be a moist hide box (see Chapter 3 for how to make a moist hide box) that offers a very humid environment for comfort and also offers a place to shed and lay eggs. Rocks similar to the kind in the *Goniurosaurus'* natural habitats—granite or limestone—may be placed in the terrarium to simulate their environments in nature. Be sure to glue multiple rocks together to prevent them from moving or falling and crushing your gecko. Shallow ceramic water and food dishes should be placed in the terrarium. The water dish should be at least 3 inches (7.6 cm) wide and should always be full and clean.

**Temperature** *Goniurosaurus* like fairly cool temperatures in the terrarium, as it is relatively cool in their natural habitat. There is, of course, some variation in natural environment, so it helps to research the specific locale using weather data to fine tune temperatures between species.

# Misting Systems and Humidifiers

*Goniusorsaurus* require high humidity in their enclosures. To maintain an acceptable relative humidity for these animals, some keepers employ misting systems and/or ultrasonic humidifiers connected to timers to provide mist several times a day. While these devices can help simplify the maintenance of gonis, they must be used cautiously.

The water produced by misting systems and humidifiers can build up in the cage and eventually reach levels that will drown your gecko. When using these devices, be sure to check the cage a few times daily. With some trial and error, you should be able to adjust the timing to prevent flooding. Having a drainage layer of small pebbles under the substrate will help, as well. The drainage layer should be 2-3 inches (5.1 to 7.6 cm) deep. Lastly, you can use a screen cage that allows the water to drain out—of course, you will need something to catch the water or it will run all over your floor. Keeping humidity high in a screen cage can be challenging, but is doable.

One other caution must be observed when using humidifiers. You should use an ultrasonic humidifier, instead of a hot or cold humidifier. Hot and cold humidifiers will cause drastic changes in the cage temperature that may harm the gecko.

There are general temperatures that work well; with *G. luii* and *G. araneus*, the author has successfully used warm season (about May to August) maximums of 82°F (27.7°C) and a nighttime drop of about 10°F (12°C). Emberton notes that the Vietnamese leopard gecko (*G. lichtenfelderi*) is more tolerant of warmer temperatures (pers. comm.). Japanese leopard geckos, as a rule, are not tolerant of temperatures above 80°F (26.7°C) as their environments are generally cooler.

In the winter months, a cooling period is necessary to simulate the natural seasonal variation experienced by *Goniurosaurus*. Kaverkin (1999) let his breeding pairs of *G. orientalis* cool to temperatures as low as 53.6°-55.4°F (12°-13°C) at night. The author let her *G. araneus* and *G. luii* cool to temperatures as low as 55-60°F(12.8-15.6°C) at night. Many gecko keepers need to do little if anything to their captive *Goniurosaurus* terrarium to achieve these temperatures because most homes maintain the same heat levels seasonally. If heating is needed, direct lighting should be avoided because these eublepharids are exclusively nocturnal and would not appreciate light in their eyes during the day. UTHs (under tank heating systems) are the most convenient option here. Be sure your UTH has an adjustable thermostat if you use one.

## Feeding

In nature, *Goniurosaurus* eat locusts, beetle larvae, caterpillars, and butterflies (Kaverkin, 1999). If you would like to feed your gecko some of the insects found in your locale, be

G. luii in a defensive pose. The tail is held up and flicked back and forth.

sure they have not been exposed to poison. In general, the Goniurosaurus feeding regimen is the same as that of the leopard gecko (see Chapter 3). Goniurosaurus should be fed at night during their active period. Extra care should be taken to make sure this sensitive eublepharid is not overwhelmed with the presence of too many uneaten food items in the enclosure.

## Captive Breeding

Goniurosaurus, if sexually mature and healthy, are fairly easy to breed in captivity. The terrarium should be checked daily for eggs during breeding season (warmer months of the

## The Knowing Nose

Hoyer and Stewart (2000) observed that *G. luii* uses scent to discriminate between prey items (swab with cricket chemicals). Evidence for the use of scent with food has been found in experiments with other eublepharids (*E. macularius* and *Coleonyx*). Similarly, the author has noticed a keen response of *E. macularius* and *Coleonyx* to food items coated with vitamin supplement versus those not coated. If a new type of food item is introduced, the chances of the gecko accepting it are greatly increased by putting a familiar supplement on the food before offering it. This knowledge comes in handy when a gecko decides to refuse its normal food regimen, perhaps needing a change in diet to re-stimulate interest. This scent food discrimination behavior is thought to be associated with active foraging and hunting modes typical of eublepharid geckos.

year) about 30 days from mating. The author and Emberton (pers. comm.) have observed their *Goniurosaurus* lay 2-3 clutches annually. Kaverkin (1999) found *G. orientalis* eggs laid in the warmest, most humid part of the terrarium. If your *Goniurosaurus* lays outside of the moist hide box, perhaps it is not moist enough and/or it is not in a warm/cool enough location. A lot of captive breeding involves trial and error in breeding setups!

A captive-bred juvenile *G. luii*. Captive-bred gonis are not as common as wild-caught ones, but are much more likely to be healthy and hardy.

Goniurosaurus eggs are typical of eublepharid eggs, oval and leathery. They should be set up in exactly the same manner as E. macularius—in incubation containers with moist substrate (see Chapter 4). The author has found 78°-79°F (25.6°C) works well as a constant incubation temperature for G. araneus and G. luii. Kaverkin successfully used 75.2°-78.8°F (24°-26°C) during the day and 69.8°-71.6°F (21°-22°C) at night with G. orientalis, which live in a cooler environment.

In about 75-85 days, hatchlings will emerge. Hatchlings should be set up in the same manner as adults, just in smaller terrariums. Plastic shoe boxes or 5-gallon (18.9 l) terrariums work well for clutchmates as long as one animal does not gain a size advantage over another. If a size difference is apparent, separate the hatchlings. Their feeding regimen is the same as that of leopard gecko hatchlings, with the addition of misting the terrarium twice daily to meet the humidity requirements of the young Goniurosaurus.

## Health Concerns

Medical concerns for Goniurosaurus are essentially the same as for E. macularius (see Chapter 5). If you decide to obtain an imported specimen, then a period of acclimation and quarantine is necessary. It is also advisable to include a visit to a veterinarian who can check for parasites by performing a fecal exam. Be sure to set up the terrarium so it is easy to clean in order to reduce the amount of fecal material present; this will better enable you to deal with parasites and bacteria.

# Chapter 9

# Cat Geckos

## by Julie Bergman

**C**at geckos (*Aeluroscalabotes felinus*) are slender-bodied, semi-arboreal geckos endemic (native) to Southeast Asia. They are very unique eublepharids, sharing few attributes or terra typica (typical living environment) within their gecko family. Kaverkin and Orlov (1998) observed that most eublepharine geckos live in arid mountain and plains regions (*Eublepharis, Hemitheconyx, Holodactylus, Coleonyx*) or in caves in Asia (*Goniurosaurus*), while *A. felinus* lives in primary rainforest.

# Experienced Hobbyists Only

Cat geckos are rare in the hobby and are not bred in any numbers. Wild-caught individuals are difficult to acclimate, usually succumbing to parasites, stress, or other factors. Because of these facts, *Aeluroscalabotes* are a poor choice for beginning gecko hobbyists.

While cat geckos have typical eublepharine characteristics such as eyes with eyelids, long thin nonadhesive toes, nocturnal active periods, and the ability to regenerate tails, they differ primarily by their prehensile tail and retractable claws. These unique claws, described by Gunther (1864), are well-suited to their semi-arboreal climbing behavior. Most keepers are unaware of the retractabilty of their claws. Noticeable and striking to keepers are the unique behaviors of this gecko that resemble those of a cat: waving of the tail, locomotion, and poses of the body.

*A. felinus* has the well-earned reputation of being very difficult to keep in captivity. Since most specimens are available as wild-caught imports, only very experienced keepers should attempt to acclimate this gecko to life in captivity. Rarely have advanced gecko keepers, such as Johnathan Emberton (East Bay Vivarium, Berkeley, CA, USA), Yuri Kaverkin, and Nikolai Orlov (1998), bred this elusive and difficult gecko in captivity. Captive-bred specimens are far more desirable than wild-caught specimens due to the high parasite load commonly carried by wild cat geckos. Quarantine and deparasitization procedures will be necessary if obtaining a wild-caught *A. felinus* (see Chapter 1).

## Natural History

Cat geckos come from Southeastern Asian regions: Indonesia (Borneo, Sumatra, Sanana/Sunana Islands), the Malaysian Peninsula, Perak, Selangor, Singapore, Sula, southern Thailand, Patani, and Sarawak (EBML Reptile database, Internet). They live a nocturnal lifestyle in primary and secondary rainforest and near cultivated fields (Nunan, 1994) ranging from 0 to 1000 m (0-0.62 miles) (ASEAN biodiversity database, Internet). This gecko has two subspecies, *Aeluroscalabotes felinus felinus* and *Aeluroscalabotes felinus multituberculatus*.

There is very sparse literature about the natural history of the cat gecko or any aspect of keeping or breeding it. Nunan (1994) remarks that a Kayan tribeswoman from Sarawak told him if her people encountered this species on their way to the rice field, they must forego the day's work and immediately return home. It was considered to be a harbinger of evil.

## Description

The cat gecko is smaller in size than the well-known leopard gecko. Of the few specimens actually documented in captivity, males ranged in length (total length) from 5.7 inches (145 mm) to 6.5 inches (165 mm) of the three pairs Kaverkin and Orlov (1998) studied and 7.3 inches (185 mm) for the individual male Nunan (1994) kept. Kaverkin and Orlov's females ranged in length from 6.7 inches (170 mm) to 7 inches (180 mm). Based on these observations, one could speculate *A. felinus* is sexually dimorphic in that females are larger than males.

Coloration of the cat gecko is primarily brown, with much variability in shade and pattern. White spotting may be present on the back and/or tail. The head is striking, with a long, triangular shape, large dark brown eyes, and a white border starting just above the lips that sharply contrasts a brown stripe just above this border. The brown stripe also varies in darkness among specimens.

This eublepharid has a slender body with a fat-storing, prehensile tail that is usually held in a curled position. Kaverkin and Orlov (1998) note that, once the tail is lost and regenerates, it does not serve the function of gripping branches as well as the original. The tail, the author as well as Kaverkin and Orlov observe, is also important as a communication device in mating, hunting, and territorial behaviors. This behavior is manifested by waving the tail back and forth. The author has also observed similar types of tail waving behavior in other eublepharids.

## Captive Care

The cat gecko has an extremely shy disposition. As a consequence, handling on a regular basis would be stressful to this gecko and is not recommended. Geckos as sensitive as *A. felinus* should be kept in a quiet room, well away from sources of noise or disturbance.

Since the research that exists on this rare eublepharid only features sexual pairs (Kaverkin and Orlov, 1998) and a single specimen (Nunan, 1994), one should keep these geckos either individually or in pairs (male and female or female and female) until more is known about how groupings of different combinations of males and females work. Males

Cat geckos are the only species of eyelid gecko that is truly arboreal.

## Hands Off

Like *Goniurosaurus*, cat geckos should be considered geckos to observe rather than hold. They are delicate geckos that easily succumb to stress.

do not get along and should not be kept together. Individuals chosen to live in the same terrarium together should be approximately the same size if female; males can be slightly smaller than females. Sex is determined in the typical eublepharine manner by looking for the presence of enlarged femoral pores and hemipenal bulges in males and the absence of hemipenal bulges in females. Due to the thinness of the tail, sexing is quite easy in *A. felinus*.

## Housing

Cat geckos seem to do well in captive environments similar to those used for *Rhacodactylus* (Emberton, pers. comm.), another gecko that also prefers cool, moist, tropical climates. A glass terrarium should be used due to the high humidity requirements of this species. The one you select should have enough floor space to provide the semi-arboreal *A. felinus* with plenty of different hiding places and enough substrate to create a suitably moist environment. Choosing a terrarium with adequate height is also important so the cat gecko can climb and hunt food. Twenty-gallon (75.7 l) terraria with sliding doors on the side are suitable and have been successfully used by Emberton (pers. comm.). Nunan (1994) used a 15-gallon (56.8 l) for an individual and Kaverkin and Orlov used 500 mm x 500 mm x 500 mm (33 gallon/113.6 l) terraria for pairs.

## Humidity

Several different techniques, separately or in combination, can be employed to keep *A. felinus* at the proper relative humidity level, which is approximately 80-90 percent. The use of a hygrometer in the terrarium is recommended.

As previously mentioned, substrate can create humidity in the terrarium. Sphagnum peat moss, coco peat, and orchid bark all work well at a depth of at least 2 inches (5 cm). The author prefers to use a 2-inch layer of sphagnum peat moss topped with a layer of fine grade orchid bark.

Potted plants also work well as a source of humidity and a place to climb. Plants should be sturdy enough for the geckos to climb and hang from as this is one of their methods of stalking food during nocturnal active periods. Philodendrons and other broad-leafed houseplants are a great choice.

A misting system may be used to do the twice-a-day misting usually needed to maintain the high level of humidity *A. felinus* needs. Nunan (1994) used a terrarium lid that was partially covered to help conserve humidity. To create additional moisture, he placed a heat pad under the terrarium that was set to come on once a day at a low temperature to heat a water dish.

## Temperature

The optimal maximum temperature range for this gecko seems to be 78.8°-84.2°F (26°-29°C), temperatures used by Nunan (1994) and Kaverkin and Orlov (1998). Emberton did not did exceed a maximum of 82°F (27.8°C). Temperatures higher than the maximum recommended temperature of 84.2°F (29°C) for any length of time pose a fatal risk and may lead to the quick demise of your gecko. Kaverkin and Orlov kept shelters at 75.2°-78.8°F (24°-26°C) at all times, and let the nighttime low temperature elsewhere in the terrarium drop as low as 66.2°-69.8°F (19°-21°C).

If your home terrarium environment cannot sustain the temperature range needed, then using a low-wattage incandescent bulb (25 watts or so) in a small fixture is a good place to start. Increase wattage as necessary. Infrared heat (heat without light) and UTHs (undertank heaters) would be an unobtrusive way to heat the nocturnal A. felinus. Make sure UTHs have adjustable thermostats. Before introducing geckos to the terrarium, accurately monitor temperatures during different times of the day with a mercury-type thermometer or one with a probe like those sold at electronics stores. If heating needs are adequate, no special lighting is needed for cat geckos, although plants will require lighting.

## Terrarium Furnishings

A comfortable environment is always crucial to the well-being of your gecko. Terrarium furnishings can provide areas that can satisfy the need for retreat, as well as appropriate places needed for breeding, shedding, etc.

As previously mentioned, plants are great additions to the cat gecko terrarium as sources of humidity. Plants also make great terrarium furniture for this tropical eublepharid to climb on.

Cat geckos require warm—not hot—and humid keeping conditions.

## No Mixing!

Because cat geckos become stressed very easily, the keeper should never house them in the same enclosure as other species of herp. Mixed-species terraria are difficult to setup correctly with hardier species; with something as prone to stress as a cat gecko, success is highly unlikely.

Multiple hiding places should be placed in warm areas of the terrarium as well (Kaverkin and Orlov, 1998). They should not be much larger in size than one or two geckos and should be completely secure, meaning the gecko can go inside and not be seen. At least one of the hiding places should be a moist hidebox (see Chapter 2). The water dish should be at least 3 inches (7.6 cm) wide and should always be full and clean.

## Feeding

Once the terrarium setup is finished and the gecko has been introduced, a feeding regimen can begin. If a female is present, set up a separate low dish for a calcium supplement. She will take what she needs to keep her bones strong and to produce good viable eggs. Keep this dish clean, dry, and full. Since cat geckos are almost exclusively nocturnal, feeding should take place at night in dim light so as not to not disturb them.

Cat geckos may be fed a dietary staple of a variety of insects, crickets, and occasional pinkie mice (Kaverkin and Orlov, 1998). They can be somewhat picky eaters. Nunan (1994) was only able to feed his male specimen about two crickets each week and an occasional spider. Food items should not be too hard-shelled with chitinous material, which is too dense for geckos to digest (for example, a beetle). A good rule of thumb is to feed a gecko a food item about 90-95 percent of its head size. For adults, this is usually a 3-week-old cricket; they are not usually interested in smaller food items.

Your gecko should be fed 2-3 times weekly. Adjust to its preference by noting how many leftover food items are present about an hour or so after feeding. It is vitally important that most of the food items in the terrarium are consumed. If much food is left over, remove it as it could attack and certainly will stress the gecko. Add a high quality reptile-specific supplement to food items with each feeding.

## Captive Breeding

Cat geckos should breed successfully and produce offspring if they are at breeding weight and thriving in their captive terrarium situation. Two leathery, oval-shaped eggs are laid about 30 days from successful mating. Kaverkin and Orlov (1998) observed females sitting on top of their eggs for 24 hours before burying them in the substrate, typically 1-1.5 inches (30-40 mm) below the surface in flower pots in the terrarium. During the time before egg burial, females were usually aggressive guarding their eggs. Emberton (pers. comm.) observed that some eggs were not always laid in moist hide boxes and desiccated quickly outside that environment. During breeding season (warmer months of the year), the terrarium should be checked daily for eggs so they do not desiccate before they can be set up in incubation medium. They should be set up for incubation in typical eublepharine style (See chapters 4 and 6).

Emberton successfully incubated multiple clutches of *A. felinus* eggs at 76°-78°F (24.4°-25.6°C). Kaverkin and Orlov (1998) used 80.6°-

82.4°F (27°-28°C) for their efforts. Both these breeding facilities used precise incubators at constant temperatures. In about 60 days, hatchlings emerged. Offspring measured approximately 3-3.2 inches (78-81 mm) and had a more diffuse pattern than the parents. Hatchlings should be set up in the exact same manner as parents, just in smaller enclosures. A typical 10-gallon (37.9 l) terrarium would do nicely for clutchmates. Food should be the same as for parents, except smaller (no bigger than the gecko's head!). It should be offered daily and removed in an hour or so if not eaten. Kaverkin and Orlov were able to get subadults to take wax worms, a good food for fattening up babies. Feed wax worms sparingly, as the young geckos may get addicted and will have to be weaned off this very tasty gecko snack! Finally, take care to separate hatchlings or subadults immediately if one gains more weight or fights with the other.

Successful captive breeding of cat geckos is still a rare event. There is much to learn about the process.

# Chapter 10

# Holodactylus

## by Tom Mazorlig

It may surprise some of you that there are eyelid geckos that hail from the African continent other than fat-tailed geckos. These geckos are two species in the genus *Holodactylus*. Only one species, H. *africanus*, is ever seen in the hobby, and it only appears rarely. These geckos are seldom imported from Africa, which is just as well, as they tend to adjust to captivity only poorly. Also, they are practically never bred. For the average hobbyist, these geckos are a poor choice of a pet or breeding subject, offering nothing to the keeper—other than rarity—that he or she wouldn't get from keeping a fat-tail, banded, or other eyelid gecko. Keeping H. *africanus* is strictly for the advanced hobbyist and professional breeder who are seeking to contribute to the collective knowledge of how to keep and breed this odd little gecko.

# Gully Geckos

When *H. africanus* appears in pet stores, it goes under several common names. Most frequently, it is called the African clawed gecko and the African fingered gecko. I find these names to be contrived and hardly distinctive. Given their propensity for living in dry river beds, I suggest using the name gully gecko for this species. The name is unique and far more descriptive than African clawed gecko—after all, most African geckos have claws. I'll be referring to them as gully geckos throughout the text.

## Description

Gully geckos are tiny lizards. The ones that show up in the hobby are rarely larger than 3 inches (7.6 cm) in total length, and the giants of the species are 4 inches (10.2 cm). They are proportioned similarly to a leopard gecko, but are more lanky. They are not quite as slender as *Coleonyx*. The genus appears to be closely related to the fat-tailed geckos, *Hemitheconyx*.

Like *Coleonyx*, the skin of gully geckos is fairly smooth, with tubercles occurring only near the vent. The heads of both males and females are quite large for their body size. They have small, spearhead-shaped tails that amount to only about a sixth of their total length.

Gully geckos are somberly colored, but have an interesting and attractive pattern. The general color is a pale nutmeg brown broken by irregular bands of a darker, sort of purplish brown. The centers of these bands are often paler than the edges. The lighter areas are extensively invaded by irregular, paler reticulations. Most individuals sport a pale stripe that runs down the spine that may be bright white and solid or quite faint and indistinct. The stripe continues to the tip of the tail, and the stripe is often bordered by dark brown on the section posterior to the pelvis. On the head, the stripe breaks up and fades, but there is usually a Y-shaped remnant just behind the eyes.

The scales on the edges of the eyelids are pale yellow, creating quite a contrast with the rest of the pattern. The bellies of gully geckos are white to pinkish white. Oddly, the outer toes and the bottoms of their feet are dark gray, while the inner toes are white. Like other eublepharines, *Holodactylus* lacks adhesive lamellae on the toes.

## Natural History

Gully geckos are found in arid regions of Africa. The natural range is fragmented, with localities in Somalia, Ethiopia, Kenya, and Tanzania. Most of the ones in the hobby are imported from Tanzania. The ground in their range is sandy to rocky. Typically, the geckos reside in gullies and depressions on the borders between deserts and savannahs, but this is a generalization. Gully geckos often dig burrows at the base of termite mounds. It is not known if termites are normally included in the diet of wild gully geckos, but captive individuals will eagerly consume the insects.

This genus is not found at great elevations. They seem to be restricted to areas that are less than 3,000 feet (0.9 km) above sea level.

The natural range of gully geckos receives very little rainfall over most of the year, but there is a short and pronounced rainy season lasting two to three months. Depending on the exact locality, the rains occur during the late spring to late summer. Over most of the range, temperatures range from highs in the low 90s (about 33.3°C) to lows in the low 60s (about 16.7°C). Gully geckos are strongly nocturnal, so it is unlikely that they would ever be exposed to temperatures that are at all close to the highs their natural range experiences. They probably stay in their burrows on the coldest evenings.

The life of a gully gecko centers around its burrow. They are proficient and enthusiastic diggers and will make extensive tunnels. Whether they forage by burrowing after subterranean invertebrates is not known but seems likely. In captivity, gully geckos will emerge from their burrows every two to three nights to forage for insects and other invertebrates. It is unknown if this pattern holds true in nature, but because the supply of insects is more variable and hunting may be unsuccessful, the geckos probably come out more often than this.

Currently, the breeding season for H. africanus is not known. It is presumed that they mate and lay eggs at the beginning of the rainy season. While there is no information about temperature-dependent sex determination in gully geckos, it is probable that they do exhibit this phenomenon, based on the fact that other members of the family exhibit it, including their closest relatives, the fat-tailed gecko.

*H. africanus* is an interesting little gecko, but it tends to fare poorly in captivity.

# The Other Species

As stated at the start of the section, there are two species of *Holodactylus*. Besides *H. africanus*, there is *H. cornii*. If *H. africanus* is considered poorly known by scientists and hobbyists, *H. cornii* is almost completely unknown. There is virtually no information available on this animal.

What is known is that *H. cornii* is similar in size and coloration to *H. africanus*. It is endemic to Somalia and probably does not overlap in range with *H. africanus*. It is believed that *H. cornii* has never been imported into the US. Since they are very similar to *H. africanus* and the ranges of the species are close to each other, there is a remote possibility that *H. cornii* has been imported but misidentified as *H. africanus*. Because they are never seen in the hobby and are barely known in nature, there will be no further discussion of *H. cornii*.

## Gully Geckos as Pets

Before purchasing a gully gecko, you should be forewarned that these are delicate captives. Even expert hobbyists and professional herpetoculturists seldom have gully geckos that live more than a few months. Little is known about what their true captive requirements are; all guidelines presented here are the best guesses we have based on the available information and the experiences of the author. If you are in doubt about your ability to keep them, you should probably choose another, more well-known species.

### Selection and Acclimation

Because gully geckos are so delicate and have such a dismal record of thriving in the terrarium, it is critical that you start with healthy individuals. All the rules presented for selecting healthy eyelid geckos discussed earlier in this book apply to gully geckos (see Chapter 1). Select individuals that have good weight and are alert. It is unlikely that you will find these animals in the average pet store, so chances are that a vendor selling gully geckos will be knowledgeable about herps and maintain adequate housing for the animals. However, if the housing seems inadequate, is dirty, or is overcrowded, seek out your geckos elsewhere.

Once you have purchased your geckos, you should take them home and immediately place them in suitable housing. Gully geckos usually suffer from heavy parasite infestations.

It is strongly recommended that you take them to a herp veterinarian within the first week or so after purchase. The veterinarian will help to establish the geckos' initial health and check for and treat any parasites—bringing a fresh stool sample will be helpful. Also because of the probable parasites, as well as any other diseases the wild-caught geckos may have, quarantine away from other herps and in fairly simple caging is recommended (see Chapter 1 for details on quarantine). Even after the quarantine is past, it is best to not house gully geckos with other species of reptile. These animals often fail to adapt to captivity, and housing them with other species will likely cause them stress, further decreasing the chances they will acclimate successfully.

## Housing

Since gully geckos are burrowing lizards, it is best to house them in a cage that will allow you to have a deep substrate. A glass aquarium will be adequate. Indeed, the transparent walls will allow you see the tunnels your lizards create, turning the terrarium into a sort of reptilian ant farm. A male and two females will be comfortable in a 10-gallon tank (38 l), but giving them more floor space is not a bad idea. You should be able to keep a group of four or five in a 20-gallon "long" (76 l).

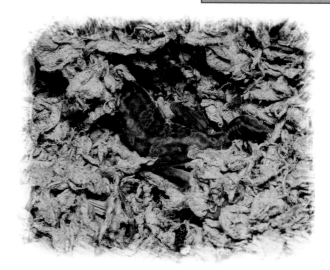

Gully geckos will spend much of their time burrowing beneath the substrate or within the hide box.

**Substrate** The best substrate for gully geckos is playground sand. You will want to make it at least 3 inches (7.6 cm) deep, although using a deeper substrate will not hurt. To make sure the lizards can form tunnels that do not collapse, you will want to keep the lower layers of sand somewhat moist. You can do this by pouring water on the sand in half the cage until it is just moist. This will set up a side of the cage that is humid and a side that is dry, allowing your geckos to move between the two.

# My Life With Gully Geckos

The information presented here on keeping *H. africanus* is based primarily on my experience keeping two trios of the species several years ago. I was fortunate enough to have one of those trios live for almost two years. During that time, I corresponded online with several other individuals who were keeping the animals, and we shared our experiences. Undoubtedly, some of the keeping techniques I used developed from their suggestions. Because so little is known about gully geckos, treat the information here as suggestions, and watch how your animals respond to their conditions. The behavior and physical condition of the geckos should be your ultimate guide on whether what you are doing is suitable or not.

Some keepers house gully geckos on a mix of sand and peat or a mix of sand and crushed coconut shell. This allows them to easily dig tunnels and keeps the humidity levels more stable. The mix should be about equal proportions sand and peat or coconut.

## Temperature and Humidity

As with other reptiles, you will want to create a temperature gradient in the terrarium. For this species, the gradient will not just be horizontal—having a cool end of the cage and a warm end—but also vertical, since the lower layers of the substrate will be significantly cooler than the surface. This gives your gecko myriad temperature and humidity choices to select from as they feel the need. The surface at the warmest spot of the terrarium should be between 87° and 90°F (30.6°-32.2°C). You can maintain this temperature with a basking light set on a timer. In a 20-gallon long (76 l), a 40- to 60-watt bulb should maintain this temperature. At night, the temperature at the surface can drop to 67°F (19.4°C) or thereabouts. Other keepers have used heat tape, heating pads, or some combination of heating devices.

Proper humidity is important for these geckos. Unfortunately, the humidity level that works best for them has yet to be determined. Again, by maintaining a humidity gradient, your geckos can select the humidity they prefer. The moist side of the cage should have a relative humidity of about 60 percent at the surface of the substrate. The lower layers will likely be more humid. Having a thermometer and a humidity gauge is strongly recommended.

## Hiding Places and Furnishings

Gully geckos spend little time above ground, so the furnishings are mainly for the benefit of the human viewer. However, a few hiding places the geckos can crawl in or under are recommended. An important point to remember is that it is quite likely the geckos will tunnel under whatever objects lie on the surface of the sand. This could lead to the objects falling on the geckos and causing injury or death. Therefore, all hiding places and other furnishings should either be lightweight or based on the bottom of the terrarium so the geckos can't burrow beneath them. I used pieces of cork bark and fragments of terra cotta flower pots with good results.

A sand substrate with a moist section makes a good substrate for a gully gecko terrarium.

If you are willing to provide proper lighting for them, live plants can be used. You can put the pots on the base of the terrarium and fill the sand around them up to the top edge of the pot. Place the plants only in the humid end of the terrarium, because watering them will add a lot of moisture to the substrate and having them at the drier end would ruin the humidity gradient. You may be able to plant the plants directly in the substrate, but I never tried this. Choose plants that do not need a lot of water. I had a small aloe and a haworthia in my gully gecko enclosure. Sansevieria should also fare well.

## Keep an Eye on Them

Because this species spends so much time beneath the sand, it is easy to miss developing health issues. Be sure to monitor the health of your geckos by observing them closely during feeding time. Be aware of their normal behaviors, and suspect a problem if their habits change suddenly. If you haven't seen your geckos on the surface for a few days, you should carefully dig them out of their burrows and look them over for any health problems.

## Food and Water

Like other eyelid geckos, gully geckos will feed on crickets, mealworms, and other insects. The insects should be gut-loaded and dusted as for leopard geckos (see Chapter 3). The ones I kept seemed to particularly enjoy wax worms and darkling beetles (the adult form of mealworms), but they completely ignored pill bugs. One keeper has reported that small roaches (Blatta orientalis is recommended) will put weight on gully geckos very quckly.

Gully geckos can eat prodigious quantities of food for their size. On average, a gully gecko can eat three or four fairly large crickets in an evening. After such a meal, the gecko will probably not eat for two days or so. Gully geckos can also eat insects that are larger than one would think; however, it is still best to err on the side of caution when it comes to the size of the insects you feed them.

Remember that these geckos are strongly nocturnal. It is best to feed them at night. In fact, it is best to feed them quite some time after the lights go out. Perhaps you should make it part of your routine to feed the geckos right before going to bed.

Keep a shallow dish of water in the cage at all times. The geckos do not drink often, but they must be allowed the option. Quite frequently, gully geckos will maintain a burrow directly under the water bowl. They will also enter the bowl and soak on occasion. Clean the water bowl as needed.

## They'll Let You Know

When I was keeping gully geckos, I found that the geckos themselves would let me know when they wanted food. If the geckos were out and roaming the surface at night, I knew they wanted food. Whenever I saw them moving about, I'd give them some insects. If they remained in their burrows, I didn't feed them that evening.

## Maintenance

You will need to pick out the feces every few days. You can use a piece of screen to sift them out of the sand. Pet stores that deal with herps often sell sand sifters for this purpose. If you are diligent about removing the feces, you

Hiding places, like broken flowerpots, are vital to a gully gecko's well-being. Several individuals will often share one hide.

will only to need to break down and clean the entire cage every six months or so. This will also depend on the number of gully geckos you have in the cage.

Note the pale color of this female; she's about to shed. Proper humidity helps ensure shedding is free of problems.

## Behavior

Other than their interesting tunnels, gully geckos exhibit a few other fascinating behaviors. When alarmed, they stand high on their legs and hold their stubby tails straight up, perpendicular to their bodies. Then they bark, usually giving their head a side-to-side shake at the same time. When stalking prey, they either hold their tail rigid or wag it like some of the other eyelid geckos do.

Gully geckos do not seem to be territorial, although I never housed more than one male per cage. I never observed any type of conflict or squabble between them. The geckos frequently rested together with their bodies in contact.

Like leopard geckos, gully geckos do not soil their lairs. The feces are usually deposited as far away from their burrows as possible.

One last behavior that gully geckos exhibit is quite strange and somewhat humorous. They will occasionally tunnel up from the substrate until just their head is above ground. When you look in the cage, it looks as though there is just a gecko head sitting on the sand.

## Breeding

Breeding gully geckos is almost never accomplished. However, they can be bred in captivity by the diligent keeper.

The first hurdle to breeding gully geckos is finding females. Most of the ones imported are males. This may mean that, in nature, the males roam further and more often than the females and are therefore collected more frequently. Second, it is not always easy to tell the males from the females. The hemipenal bulge of the males may not be large enough to distinguish them from the females. The most accurate way of sexing gully geckos is to use a

# From the Breeder

**Very few Individuals have succeeded in breeding *H. africanus*; I was not one of them. The information in this section primarily comes from Marcus Quesada, who bred gully geckos on a few occasions. I am grateful to Marcus for providing me with this information and allowing me to use it in this book.**

magnifying glass to look at the femoral pores, which will be larger and more numerous on the males. If you are in doubt when purchasing gully geckos and don't have a magnifying glass, select those with the largest hemipenal bulges (hopefully males) and those that appear to lack hemipenal bulges (hopefully females).

Like many other herps, a seasonal change in temperatures will help trigger breeding in H. *africanus*. It is possible that just the change in temperature in your home over the course of a year will be enough to stimulate reproduction. Good results breeding gully geckos have come when the cage temperature was allowed to drop down to a range of 78° to 82°F (about 25.6°-27.8°C) for about three months. Hobbyists who have tried to hibernate these geckos at temperatures in the 50s (about 10°-15°C) have for the most part ended up with dead geckos.

Shortly after the temperatures return to normal, the geckos will breed. They seem to prefer to mate in their hiding places but not actually in their burrows. Interestingly, female gully geckos will tend to isolate themselves from the others when gravid. They will take up solo residence in a burrow or hiding place. They also become much less active.

Gully geckos lay one to two eggs and can lay a few clutches per

Male gully geckos (right) have large hemipenal bulges and small spurs near the vent, while females (left) do not. However, sometimes the difference is subtle.

season. Usually, the first clutch will contain two eggs and the second contains one, but there is some variation. The eggs are very small, about the size of a pea. They are not quite as soft and flexible as other eublepharid eggs, appearing to be more calcified.

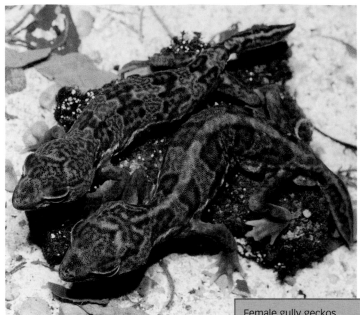

Female gully geckos tend to be more slender and have proportionally smaller heads than the males.

Successful incubation has occurred by setting the eggs up on moist perlite (be careful as telling the difference between the eggs and the perlite can be a challenge) at temperatures ranging from 82° to 84°F (27.8°-28.9°C). To moisten the perlite, saturate it completely and drain it in a colander. Thereafter, maintain the humidity by misting every week or so. When you incubate like this, the eggs will hatch in about six weeks.

The baby gully geckos are tiny—at most, half an inch long. They will shed in about two days and then begin eating. They will eat pinhead crickets and baby roaches. You could also try fruit flies, rice flour beetles, and termites. They grow slowly but steadily when given enough food.

## Conclusion

Gully geckos are interesting and challenging lizards for the specialist hobbyist. There are many facets of their biology that are still mysterious, so the hobbyist has a lot of room to make contributions to understanding these charming creatures. However, because they tend to do so poorly in captivity, they should only be purchased by those hobbyists and professional herpetoculturists who are dedicated to giving them superlative care.

# Leopard Geckos

Autumn, K., and D.F. DeNardo. 1995. Behavioral Thermoregulation Increases Growth Rate in a Nocturnal Lizard. *Journal of Herpetology* 29(2):157-162.

Balsai, Michael. 1993. Leopard Geckos. *Reptile and Amphibian Magazine* March/April, 2-13.

Bartlett, Dick. 1996. Eublepharines: Let's Talk. *Reptiles* April, 48-67.

Bertoni, Ribello. 1995. Banded Geckos. *Reptile and Amphibian Magazine* March/April, 60-66.

Black, Adam. 2003. Starting a Lizard Breeding Project. *Reptiles* 11(12): 78-89.

Black, Jesse. 1997. Keeping and Breeding Leopard Geckos. *Reptiles*, 5(3): 10-18.

Conant, Roger, and J.T. Collins. 1998. *A Field Guide to Reptiles and Amphibians Eastern and Central North America*. 3rd ed. Boston and New York: Houghton Mifflin Company, 616 pps.

Coomber, P. David Crews, and Francisco Gonzalez-Lima. 1997. Independent Effects of Incubation Temperature and Gonadal Sex on the Volume and Metabolic Capacity of Brain Nuclei in the Leopard Gecko (*Eublepharis macularius*), a Lizard With Temperature-Dependent Sex Determination. *Journal of Comparative Neurology* 380: 409-421.

Crews, David. 1994. Animal Sexuality. *Scientific American* 270: 108-114.

DeNardo, D. F., and G. Helminski. 2001. The Use of Hormone Antagonists to Inhibit Reproduction in the Lizard *Eublepharis macularius*. *Journal of Herpetological Medicine and Surgery* 11(3):4-7.

de Vosjoli, Philippe. 1990. *The Right Way to Feed Insect-Eating Lizards*. Lakeside, CA: Advanced Vivarium Systems, 32pps.

de Vosjoli, Philippe, Roger Klingenberg, Ron Tremper, and Brian Viets. 2004. *The Leopard Gecko Manual*. Irvine, CA: Advanced Vivarium Systems, 96 pps.

de Vosjoli, Philippe, Ron Tremper, and Roger Klingenberg. 2005. *The Herpetoculture of Leopard Geckos*. Advanced Visions Inc., 259 pps.

Frantz, Steven L. 1993. In Search of Tokage Modoki, the Japanese Leopard Gecko (*Goniurosaurus* (*Eublepharis*) *kuroiwae*). *The Vivarium* 4/5: 21-24.

Hiduke, Joe and Meadow Gaines. 1996. Central American Banded Geckos: *Coleonyx Mitratus*. *Reptiles* October, 76-87.

Hiduke, Joe and Bill Brant. 2003. Leopards and Beardies. 2003 *Annual Reptiles USA* vol. 8: 94-101.

Kluge, A. G. 1987. Cladistics Relationships in the Gekkonoidea (Squamata: Sauria). *Mis. Publ. Mus. Univ. Michigan.* 173: 1-54.

Madge, David. 1985. Temperature and Sex Determination in Reptiles with References to Chelonians. *Testudo* Vol. 2(3).

Puente, Lyle. 2000. *The Leopard Gecko*. New York, NY: Howell Book House, Wiley Inc, 119 pps.

Stebbins, Robert C. 2003. *A Field Guide to Western Reptiles and Amphibians*. 3rd ed. Boston and New York: Houghton Mifflin Company, 533 pps.

Tremper, Ron. 1997. Designer Leopard Geckos. *Reptiles* 5(3): 16.

Tremper, Ron. 2000. Designer Leopard Geckos. *Reptiles* 8(3): 10-17.

Tremper, Ron. 2005. Orange Is In! *Reptiles* 13(3): 28-36.

Viets, B. E. 2004. Incubation, Temperature and Hatchling Sex and Pigmentation. in *The Leopard Gecko Manual*. Irvine, CA: Advanced Vivarium Systems. 96 pps.

Vella, Jay. 2000. The Blizzard Lizard. *Reptiles* 8(3): 24-29.

Wibbels, T. and David Crews. 1995. Steroid-Induced Sex Determination at Incubation Temperatures Producing Mixed Sex ratios in a Turtle With TSD. *General and Comparative Endocrinology*.100: 53-60.

Wright, Kevin. 1998. Cryptosporidia: New Hope on the Horizon. *Reptile and Amphibian Magazine* 55,32-36

# Cat Geckos

Kaverkin, Y.I. and N.L. Orlov. 1998. Captive Breeding of Cat Geckos, *Aeluroscalabotes felinus*. *Dactylus* 3 (2):87-89.

Nunan, J. 1994. "In the Spotlight" *Aeluroscalabotes felinus* (Gunther, 1864). *Dactylus* 2 (3): 107-108.

Asian Regional Centre for Biodiversity Conservation and Information Sharing Service:

http://arcbc.org/cgi-bin/abiss.exe/spd?tx=RE&spd=13

EBML Reptile Database:

http://www.embl-heidelberg.de/~uetz/families/Gekkonidae.html

# *Goniurosaurus*

Bragg, W.K., J.D. Fawcett, T.B. Bragg, B.E. Viets. 2000. Nest-Site Selection in Two Eublepharid Gecko Species with Ttemperature-Dependent Sex and One With Genotypic Sex Determination. *Zoological Journal of the Linnean Society* 69: 319-332.

 Cooper, W.E . and J.J. Habegger. 2000. Lingual and Biting Responses by Some Eublepharid and Gekkonid Geckos. *Journal of Herpetology* 34 (3) 360-368.

Goris, R.C. and M. Maeda. 2004. *Guide to the Amphibians and Reptiles of Japan*. Malabar, Florida: Krieger Publishing Company.

Grismer, L.L., B.E. Viets and L.J. Boyle. 1999. Two New Continental Species of *Goniurosaurus* (Squamata: Eublepharidae) with a Phylogeny and Evolutionary Classification of the Genus. *Journal of Herpetology* 33: 382-393.

Grismer, L.L. 2000. *Goniurosaurus* murphyi Orlov and Darevsky: A Junior Synonym of *Goniurosaurus lichtenfelderi* Mocqard. *Journal of Herpetology* 34 (3): 486-488.

Grismer, L.L. 2002. *Goniurosaurus*: Ancient gekkos of the Far East. *Gekko* 3(1): 22-28.

Grismer, L.L., S. Haitao, N.I. Orlov, and N.B. Anajeva. 2002. A New Species of *Goniurosaurus* (Squamata: Eublepharidae) from Hainan Island, China. *Journal of Herpetology* 36 (2): 217-224.

Henkel, F.W. and W. Schmidt. 2004. *Professional Breeders Series: Geckos – All Species in One Book.*: Frankfurt am Main: Edition Chimaira.

Kaverkin, Yuri. (1999). Tokage Modoki: Those Wonderful Geckos of the Ryukyu Archipelago. *Gekko* 1(1): 42-46.

Orlov, N.I. and I.S. Daresky. 1999. Description of a New Mainland Species of *Goniurosaurus* Genus from the North-Eastern Vietnam. *Russian Journal of Herpetology* 6: 72-78.

Werner, Y., L. Takahasi, Y. Yasukawa, and H. Ota. 2004. The Varied Foraging Mode of the Subtropical Gecko *Goniurosaurus kuroiwae orientalis*. *Journal of Natural History* 38: 119-134.

EBML Reptile Database:
http://www.embl-heidelberg.de/~uetz/families/Gekkonidae.html

Red List of Threatened Reptiles of Japan
http://www.biodic.go.jp/english/rdb/red_reptiles.txt

## CLUBS AND SOCIETIES

**Amphibian, Reptile & Insect Association**
Liz Price
23 Windmill Rd
Irthlingsborough
Wellingborough NN9 5RJ
England

**American Society of Ichthyologists and Herpetologists**
Maureen Donnelly, Secretary
Grice Marine Laboratory
Florida International University
Biological Sciences
11200 SW 8th St.
Miami, FL 33199
Telephone: (305) 348-1235
E-mail: asih@fiu.edu
www.asih.org

**The Global Gecko Association**
c/o Leann Christenson
1155 Cameron Cove Circle
Leeds, Alabama 35094
E-mail: membership@gekkota.com
http://www.gekkota.com/

**Society for the Study of Amphibians and Reptiles (SSAR)**
Marion Preest, Secretary
The Claremont Colleges
925 N. Mills Ave.
Claremont, CA 91711
Telephone: 909-607-8014
E-mail: mpreest@jsd.claremont.edu
www.ssarherps.org

## VETERINARY RESOURCES

**Association of Reptile and Amphibian Veterinarians**
P.O. Box 605
Chester Heights, PA 19017
Phone: 610-358-9530
Fax: 610-892-4813
E-mail: ARAVETS@aol.com
www.arav.org

## RESCUE AND ADOPTION SERVICES

**ASPCA**
424 East 92nd Street
New York, NY 10128-6801
Phone: (212) 876-7700
E-mail: information@aspca.org
www.aspca.org

**Las Cruces Reptile Rescue**
www.awesomereptiles.com/lcrr/rescueorgs.html

**New England Amphibian and Reptile Rescue**
www.nearr.com

**Petfinder.com**
www.petfinder.org

**Reptile Rescue, Canada**
http://www.reptilerescue.on.ca/

**RSPCA (UK)**
Wilberforce Way
Southwater
Horsham, West Sussex RH13 9RS
Telephone: 0870 3335 999
www.rspca.org.uk

# WEBSITES

**Fattailgecko.com**
www.fattailgecko.com

**Gecko Network**
http://www.geckonetwork.com/mainsec.htm

**GeckoWorld**
www.geckoworld.com

**Gexfiles**
http://www.gexfiles.com/

**Herp Station**
http://www.petstation.com/herps.html

**Kingsnake.com**
http://www.kingsnake.com

**Leopard Gecko Care**
http://www.anapsid.org/leopardgek.html

**Melissa Kaplan's Herp Care Collection**
http://www.anapsid.org/

**Reptile Forums**
http://reptileforums.com/forums/

**The Reptile Rooms**
http://www.reptilerooms.org/

# MAGAZINES

***Herp Digest***
www.herpdigest.org

***Reptiles***
P.O. Box 6050
Mission Viejo, CA 92690
www.animalnetwork.com/reptiles

***Reptilia***
Salvador Mundi 2
Spain-08017 Barcelona
Subscripciones-subscriptions@reptilia.org

---

## *Photo Credits:*

J. Balzarini: 8, 10, 60, 73
R. D. Bartlett: 11, 44, 68, 76, 92, 94, 95, 102, 109
Adam Black (courtesy of The Gourmet Rodent): 13 (top), 45, 47, 52, 54, 57, 62 (bottom), 64, 65, 74, 77
Allen Both: 66
I. Francais: 22, 27, 29, 30, 39, 40, 51
Paul Freed: 18, 53, 99, 100, 105, 107
James Gerholdt: 15, 58

Erik Loza: 24
G. and C. Merker: 1, 13 (bottom), 17, 21, 25, 38, 42, 49, 56, 62 (top), 82, 83, 85, 86, 87, 88, 89, 90, 97, 101, and cover
J. Merli: 36
K. H. Switak: 69, 80,
M. Walls: 75, 110, 113, 115, 117, 119, 120, 121
Christian Yule: 70

# Index

Note: Boldface numbers indicate illustrations.